WITNESS
TO A CITY

David Miller (signature)

WITNESS TO A CITY

DAVID MILLER'S TORONTO

DAVID MILLER AND DOUGLAS ARROWSMITH
PHOTOGRAPHS BY JEFF DAVIDSON

Cormorant Books

To Joan Bunn:
with loving memory
of my mum, Joan.

_DM_ (signature)

Sept 23, 2011

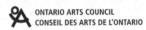

The publisher gratefully acknowledges the support of the Canada Council for the Arts
and the Ontario Arts Council for its publishing program. We acknowledge the
financial support of the Government of Canada through the
Canada Book Fund for our publishing activities.

Printed and bound in Canada

LIBRARY AND ARCHIVES CANADA CATALOGUING IN PUBLICATION

Miller, David, 1958–
Witness to a city : David Miller's Toronto / David Miller, Douglas Arrowsmith;
photographs by Jeff Davidson.

ISBN 978-1-897151-80-8

1. Toronto (Ont.) — Social life and customs — 21st century — Anecdotes.
2. Cultural pluralism — Ontario — Toronto — Anecdotes.
3. Toronto (Ont.) — Anecdotes.
I. Arrowsmith, Doug, 1968– II. Davidson, Jeffery John, 1966–
III. Title. IV. Title: David Miller's Toronto.

FC3097.3.M54 2010   971.3'54105   C2009-907216-5

Cover design: Angel Guerra/Archetype
Interior text design: Tannice Goddard/Soul Oasis Networking
Cover photograph by Jeff Davidson
Printer: Friesens

Mixed Sources
Cert no. SW-COC-001271
© 1996 FSC
FSC

The text of this book is printed on 100% post-consumer waste recycled paper.

CORMORANT BOOKS INC.
215 SPADINA AVENUE, STUDIO 230, TORONTO, ON CANADA M5T 2C7
www.cormorantbooks.com

To Jill, and our children, Julia and Simon,
who have unfailingly supported me
throughout my tenure as an elected official.

CONTENTS

INTRODUCTION

The moment is etched on my mind. The new Bamboo restaurant at the waterfront was packed with what seemed like thousands of Torontonians — environmentalists, advocates for social justice and integrity in government, transit supporters, small business people, and, of course, opponents of the island airport. New Democrats, Liberals, Red Tories, and unaffiliated voters wildly celebrating the fact that I had just won the mayoralty of Canada's largest city with forty-three per cent of the vote — me, the longshot candidate from High Park who started at below eight per cent in the polls.

But it is not the victory itself that I remember so clearly: it is the moment I first saw my children in that room. I was on stage with my wife, Jill, holding hands, as we had been most of the day as we travelled the entire city thanking supporters and urging them to get out to vote. I looked up, over the cheering crowd, to the balcony and just happened to see Julia and Simon (then aged eight and six) looking down, drinking in the wild celebrations. I was so excited that I grabbed Jill and we both waved. The photograph of Jill and me smiling widely and waving to our children was the cover of *The Globe and Mail* the next day, with the headline "Impeccable Victory, Impeccable Mandate."

Perhaps this moment is so clear to me because of my own family history. I had no brother, no sister, no father — but a remarkably strong and resilient mother. As a result, the role of being a father, and a husband, is both unfamiliar and incredibly important to me.

⟞⟝

EARLY YEARS

MY MUM, JOAN, was born in East Anglia in England in 1919, the youngest of three, with two older brothers — Raymond and George. Both of my uncles have played influential roles in my life, as did my grandfather, George Albert Green, whom I lived with in England as a young boy. George was English and his wife, Anne, Irish, likely a bit unusual at the time.

Probably the biggest thing that happened in my mum's early life was that her mother, Anne, died far too young, when Joan was fourteen. Joan always referred to her as "my sweet darling mother" and felt strongly that she had been worked to death by the traditional household responsibilities of an English woman at that time. As would be expected, Mum assumed many of those responsibilities as a young woman — she told me more than once that she resolved then never to be a man's servant again.

In the Great Depression, in a working-class family, everyone who could had a job — and everyone was frugal. Granddad worked for the London and Northeastern Railway; Uncle George married young and became a meter reader with the electric company in Ipswich; Uncle Ray enlisted in the Royal Navy (where he promptly became nicknamed "Jim"), and Mum attended teachers' college at Avery Hill College in London.

Her first job was teaching at the public school in Dagenham, London. She started in the 1939–40 school year, a tragic year to be in London. Mum began working in this very working-class neighbourhood at the height of the Blitz, in a place that was heavily bombed by Germany because of the local car factory. Combined with Uncle Jim's experiences in the war, teaching the youngest children in a neighbourhood destroyed by bombs made her a lifelong advocate for peace. I think it is hard to understand that anti-war passion unless you have experienced the complete futility and horror of war — as my family did.

Postwar, both Mum and Uncle Jim emigrated to Canada — Mum to teach in Halifax, Jim to enlist in the Royal Canadian Navy, after a few other jobs, where he served with distinction until the 1960s.

The next part of my mum's story is one she didn't share because she was so private; suffice to say that Joan Green emigrated to the United States, met Joe Miller, became Mrs. Joan Miller, and that Joe Miller died of leukemia very shortly after I was born. Mum then took me back to England, where she had obtained employment as a headmistress of a local school in a tiny farming village, Thriplow, in Cambridgeshire. My first memories are of living in Thriplow with Mum and Granddad.

I loved Thriplow. We lived in the school; across the street was Parker's Eggs where "Auntie" May and "Auntie" Nell took care of the free-range chickens and a few sheep. They also had an egg-vending machine — still the only one I have ever seen.

What else was in the village? The church, of course — all was run by the Church of England and we went every week. Also in the village were the landed gentry and their magnificent property, the workers' cottages, council houses (where my friends John, Colin, and Gary Betts lived), a small middle-class subdivision of ten houses or so, a shop, a pub, and a working blacksmith. That was about it.

But we had fun. The Betts and I, and older boys who were farmers' or workers' sons, played soccer and cricket, played in the streams and the fields, and were generally free to do as we wished. With one exception: every night my mother corrected my English — I spoke like a local farmers' son and she insisted, every night, that I speak the Queen's English. When I protested that I wanted to speak like my friends she would say, "If you sound like a farmer, that is all you will be." For a working-class woman, the idea of her only child's future being limited by his accent was unacceptable. She was so determined that, in 1966, with the aid of a scholarship I had won, Mum sent me to a private school in Cambridge (the Perse) instead of her own school so I could have the education she thought was essential. This would prove to be a pattern in her life — making significant sacrifices so I could have the education she thought was necessary to give me opportunity.

Mum, Granddad, and I had holidays — generally we went to the sea — by train to Folkestone, or in the summer to Butlin's Holiday Camp where loudspeakers would play "Oh What a Beautiful Morning" and we would eat at long group tables with other holidaying families. At home Granddad loved to make his toast over the coal fireplace using a long fork, and would roll his own cigarettes from tinned tobacco. He took great joy from his vegetable garden in the back, and was none too pleased when he would catch me playing with my toy soldiers in the potato plants.

In February 1967 my grandfather died, and Mum decided to move to Canada, to Ottawa, to be near Uncle Jim. Canada was searching for teachers at the time, and Mum was able to find a position with the Ottawa public school board. By this point, Uncle Jim had retired from the navy and had become a kind of Labour Arbitrator in the federal public service. Like many newcomers, we lived with our relatives at first, in the basement of Uncle Jim and Aunt Jane's house in the Alta Vista neighbourhood of Ottawa.

Also like many newcomers, my mother struggled to get accepted into her new job. Despite having taught for nearly thirty years, and having a job, the Ottawa School Board at first insisted that she wasn't qualified to teach in Canada because she did not have a qualification that was impossible for non-Canadians to have: grade thirteen, which did not exist outside Ontario, let alone Canada. I can still remember her outrage at being told that a two-year program at teachers' college at the University of London was not good enough to teach in Canada. Ultimately, she was able to obtain a certificate of equivalency, but the experience has left me with a strong understanding of how frustrating it still is for many newcomers to our country who cannot get their qualifications recognized.

My mother taught at elementary schools in Ottawa, always taking night and summer university courses in order to get her degree (which she ultimately received in 1975 at the age of fifty-six) and the equivalency of a master's in library science, allowing her to become a teacher-librarian. She had taught me to read before I attended school — leading to a lifelong love of reading. I had another lifelong love, though: sports.

I attended my local public schools in Ottawa — Arch Street Public and Hawthorne Elementary — and, after a difficult first year, was generally happy, except for one big gap: sports. I could play hockey — and played endless games of ball hockey with the local boys — but having started at the age of ten meant I struggled, unlike the English sports of soccer and cricket that I had left behind. I really missed the competition and the skill that I'd enjoyed. At the same time, my mum was concerned (although I did not know this until years later) that I did not have the presence of men in my life; she was used to a British tradition of boys attending all-boys' schools.

This came to a head in 1971 due to the delivery of a copy of the *Canadian Magazine* with the Saturday *Ottawa Citizen*. The magazine had a cover photograph of a group of very happy Upper Canada College boys playing cricket. Cricket! Now there was a sport. I immediately said, "Mum, I want to go there." Of course, going to a school like Upper Canada College on a teacher's salary (especially low because she did not yet have a degree) was absolutely impossible. But Mum thought it was very important for an adolescent boy to have male role models, and made sufficient enquiries to determine that UCC and other schools had some scholarship spaces. She also found out about two lesser-known independent schools — Lakefield College School and Stanstead, both of which seemed very welcoming.

In the spring of 1972 I sat for the scholarship exams. Although I was accepted into all three schools, only Lakefield and Stanstead offered scholarships. We visited Lakefield in the spring of 1972 and were impressed — Mum with the small class sizes, its accessibility by bus from Ottawa, and the sense of rugged Canadian outdoors. Me? They had cricket. I was happy. Mum? Delighted — so delighted, in fact, that she took on two additional part-time jobs to help pay the remaining fees.

I started LCS (the Grove, as it is known to its alumni and friends) in September 1972. While I was very nervous at first, I quickly fit in, doing well academically and playing soccer, hockey, and cricket, and being known as "Miller," as was the school habit.

At Thanksgiving of grade nine, Lewis, Greenwood, Morrison, and I went on the school canoe trip to Algonquin Park. Our group included the headmaster, Terry Guest, and the Biology teacher, Ken Burns, likely because Lewis, Morrison, and I were all new boys. It was an incredibly beautiful fall day when we started from Smoke Lake, doing the several day circuit through Lake Louisa and back to Smoke. That night the temperature dropped and we woke up to snow, wind, and, when the snow let up, a bitterly cold and driving rain. Unfortunately, perhaps because we were new boys, or simply because no one had advised our parents that we needed rain gear (readily available from the school shop "Chiefs" located deep in the basement of the Grove and run by a former chief petty officer who terrified grade nine students), the four of us had to endure being soaked to the skin and frozen. I still remember how cold it felt — but I can also remember something else: the incredible sense of pride and accomplishment we all felt overcoming those challenges.

On one very long portage, carrying a canvas and leather pack that, soaking wet, probably weighed as much as I did, I simply kept going — mostly to stay warm — despite needing a break hundreds of yards before the end. I was the first one over, and found a dry place to wait. Mr. Guest came a few minutes later, carrying a canoe — he said "Miller, that was quick. Did you stop?" When I said no, he said, "That takes guts." What an incredible thing for a headmaster to say to a skinny, awkward new boy, the scholarship kid at a school with students from families like Eaton and Labatt, Demerais and Irving. Ever since, I have always believed in my own capacity to endure and overcome challenges.

Lakefield formed me in other ways. The school also trained us to be leaders — teaching older boys to set an example, and requiring grade thirteen students to assume leadership positions. I was selected to be the Head Boy, and also captained the rugby and soccer teams. One of the special things about Lakefield was that the school encouraged you to participate in many extracurricular activities — so I had a chance to debate, act, and sing in the choir. I was also an altar boy — as an Anglican school, we attended chapel six days a week. The values of social justice taught by the church were an important part of our life, as was the lusty singing of hymns like "The Lord of the Dance" and "Jerusalem." I still find great peace in an Anglican church when wonderful choral and organ music flows over me.

I loved choir — even though singing is not a great strength of mine. In grade thirteen I somehow landed a solo. I will never forget how frustrated the choirmaster used to get with me in rehearsals — or what happened when my mum came to watch. She told the choirmaster afterwards, "A solo! I never would have believed it. My David, a solo." To which Mr. Thompson replied, dead seriously, "A pure act of charity on my part, Mrs. Miller."

I developed other loves at Lakefield; I read voraciously, particularly offbeat books like those by Kurt Vonnegut and Joseph Heller. I learned to love Shakespeare, Monty Python, and Bruce Springsteen, who I saw play in Maple Leaf Gardens in 1975 on the *Born to Run* tour.

In grade thirteen, Dr. Rosalind Barker, our English teacher, was responsible for helping us with our university applications. She had done graduate work in the United States, and I knew from Mum that my dad had studied at Brown University, an Ivy League school in Rhode Island. When I mentioned it to Mrs. Barker, she encouraged me to apply. She also said something that would ultimately shape my life: "Miller, if you are going to apply to an Ivy League school, you should apply to Harvard." The application required a lot of work — essays, references, an interview — but I worked hard and sent in the complete application to both Harvard and Brown, as well as Queen's, University of Toronto, and Waterloo — with no expectation at all that I would get in to any U.S. university.

In May, a large brown envelope came from Harvard — on a day I had no class in the third period when mail was usually delivered. As a result, I happened to be in the mail room and saw the envelope — we all knew rejection letters were small white envelopes. I ripped it open and it was an acceptance letter — a significant scholarship offer and the promise of a job. I phoned Mum at work and called her out of class — the only time ever — and told her the news. "Mum, I got into Harvard." "Harvard. Harvard! Harvard!" "Mum, it's very expensive, I don't have to go." I will never forget her reply: "It's only money, David, it is only money."

The decision was made, and in the fall of 1977 I arrived at Harvard, scholarship in hand. My first job at Harvard: dorm crew (cleaning the toilets). I didn't mind; I had had previous jobs at Lakefield in the summer, and ultimately worked at various part-time positions all through university. In most of the summers I went to Alberta and paved roads; it was hard but well-paid work.

Despite being at a private all-boys' school, I had developed a keen sense of social justice, and was very curious about why there were such extremes of wealth and opportunity in our society. I was good at math, and after freshman year decided to make economics my major. I joined the rugby club, and in sophomore year became the co-captain. I also met, and fell in love with, my first girlfriend, and began to experience how free one could be in university. The results weren't good — I did well in my economics studies, but socializing and rugby caught up with me in my other courses and my grades were terrible. I learned a bitter lesson that if I was going to do well I had to work hard — I wasn't nearly smart enough to coast through Harvard.

As a junior and senior, I learned to apply myself and study hard and well, and my grades benefited as a result. I ultimately graduated in 1981 with second-class honours — in Harvard terms, *Magna cum laude*. At the same time, we had tremendous success on the rugby field, being undefeated for three seasons, and going all the way to the 1981 U.S. national championship, which we narrowly lost to Berkeley in sudden death overtime. Rugby taught me camaraderie, how to be a leader when needed, and how to simply be a teammate when that was more important. It taught me how to win and how to accept defeat. Those lessons were to prove invaluable in my careers as a lawyer and as an elected official.

POLITICS

I AM OFTEN asked, "How did you get into politics?"

The answer is both simple and complicated, and probably goes back to 1967, the year we came to Canada. Before we came, I did not know much, if anything, about Canada. In fact, when my mother told me we were emigrating, I said, "Why are we going to America, Mummy?"

I had been to London a few times, but otherwise knew only my village, Thriplow; Cambridge, where I went to school; and Ipswich, where my Uncle George and Aunt Donza lived.

We landed in Canada in August. My Uncle Jim met us at the boat in Montreal, and the next day took us to Expo '67. It was incredible — the monorail going through the U.S. dome, the exhibits from all the countries, people speaking every language in the world, Moshe Safdie's Habitat, the rides — I had never seen anything like it. I still didn't really know what Canada was, but I liked the sense of excitement, the apparent belief that anything was possible.

That sense of excitement continued in Ottawa. The Canadian government had had a huge building program for the Centennial, and living in Ottawa you quickly became aware of the importance of the government to these initiatives — and equally rapidly aware of its members. I remember very clearly Pierre Trudeau becoming prime minister and the incredible sense of optimism in this country — that by coming together through our government, we could accomplish anything. My mum simply loved him — although she was a Labour supporter in England, and would often vote NDP in other elections, she was a confirmed Trudeau supporter.

I also saw another side of Canada in my grade seven and eight school, Hawthorne Elementary. My family was rare at that time — I was an only child of a single mum, living in an apartment building. Most of the kids at Hawthorne were living in single-family homes in a resolutely middle-class neighbourhood. There were a few, however, who were not very well off at all — and lived in Ontario Housing. I saw at Hawthorne that the kids from middle-class families who got into serious trouble had their parents called to the school — whereas the poor kids had the police.

I do not know whether it was this experience, the education system in England (which, at the time, still had the "11 plus" test that tended to send working-class kids to trade schools, while upper-class kids would go to private schools, even if they failed), or my upbringing, but by grade eight I had a clear sense that the world was not just. In Ottawa, justice came through politics. I was impressed by the passion and arguments of David Lewis, the NDP leader, and in the model parliament of grade eight, became the NDP leader.

My views were reinforced at Lakefield and Harvard, and I continued to be interested in politics — but as a way of understanding the world, and seeking justice. I remember one incident very clearly at Harvard. My residence, Quincy House, had a house committee (sort of a student government except that everyone in the residence was a member) that met on Sunday nights. Harvard also had a tradition of "tables," at which students with a common interest had lunch or dinner, usually with a large sign to announce it: French table, for example, where people would speak in French. One day the guest table was the gay table, and had a large sign that said "gay table." It caused some controversy, as homophobia was far more prevalent in 1979 than today, and became a topic of discussion at the next house committee meeting. Two students I knew well raised the issue of "signs" and asked the house committee to ban signs from the dining room. It was clear what they meant, but there was embarrassed shuffling and a discussion about the merits, or not, of signs.

I was infuriated by the hypocrisy of it all, and, when it was my turn to speak, said, with considerable passion, "I am the captain of the rugby club. We speak directly. You don't mean to ban signs, or you would have said something about all the other signs that have been in the dining room. What you mean is to ban gays. Why don't we debate that instead — Quincy House banning gays? I won't support that but at least it would be an honest debate." The proposal was quickly abandoned — and I learned the effectiveness of standing up and naming it when something was wrong.

By junior year at Harvard this sense of justice, together with much better grades, allowed me to think about a way to seek justice — by attending law school.

In senior year I began the process of applying to law school. Having been born in the United States, and having very good grades from Harvard, and an excellent LSAT, I knew that I would have a chance to get into a good U.S. law school. But I did not want to live in the United States. Ronald Reagan had just been elected president; as an economics student, I knew that his economic policies were ludicrous. Anyone remotely progressive found his social policies to be frightening. I wanted to live in a country with socially progressive policies, like national health care, and progressive environmental policies (Reagan had famously said that acid rain came from trees), and chose to return to Canada and attend law school at an excellent university, the University of Toronto.

Although I did not earn one of the rare scholarships to the U of T Faculty of Law, the low tuition fees, OSAP, and summer work allowed me to afford law school. Having seen the movie *Paper Chase* right before attending U of T, I was a little intimidated by law school at first, but soon grew impatient wanting to practise law. In law school, in pursuit of justice, I worked for Downtown Legal Services and for the Union of Injured Workers, helping people who could not afford a lawyer. In the summers I was fortunate to obtain a position at the prominent Bay Street firm Aird & Berlis, where the lieutenant governor of Ontario, John Black Aird, was the name partner. I subsequently articled at Aird & Berlis, was hired as a lawyer, and in 1989 became a partner at the age of thirty.

By then I was living my dream job. I was a litigation lawyer working in the areas of immigration, employment, and corporate litigation. I had, of course, remained interested in politics — my opinions were as loud as anyone's in the pub after a game with the Saracens rugby club, and I had joined the NDP and volunteered on a few election campaigns knocking on doors, but that was about it. However, Aird & Berlis had me work on one client that made me think about politics in a much more practical and immediate way: the Toronto Islands Residents Association.

When I articled in 1984/85, the Progressive Conservative provincial government had just ended the long dispute between the residents of Toronto Islands and the regional government of the time (Metro) by passing legislation promoted by Conservative cabinet minister Larry Grossman, Bill 119, that allowed the residents to stay. The legislation required the residents to pay market rent for their homes, which resulted in an arbitration between the city, Metro, and the residents association to determine the rent. I worked on the arbitration, and in doing so, became deeply immersed in the history and reality of the Islands and the extraordinary way its residents had been mistreated, and the extremely effective way they worked to keep a small residential community on the Islands.

As a lawyer, the firm assigned me literally hundreds of cases of Island residents being prosecuted by either the city or Metro. The situation was bizarre. The residents had either built their homes or bought them from someone who had built them — simple structures that generally started out as tents. Many had deteriorated during the long fight to preserve the residential neighbourhoods because the Metro government, the landlord of the land leases (the residents owned the buildings and had land leases with Metro) had refused to consent to building permits. After the province passed legislation allowing the neighbourhoods to stay, Metro still refused to give its consent to permits necessary for repairs to the buildings.

At the same time, the city supported the neighbourhoods, believing, correctly, that small residential communities kept the Islands safer and more alive. The city also had an obligation to enforce property standards and the building code. The result of two governments supporting the residents and one opposing was an outrage — Kafka could have used it as the background for a book.

Under provincial legislation, the residences were legal. Their local government, the City of Toronto, wanted them to stay, and wanted the houses to be brought up to code. Metro refused to accept this, and by a legal manoeuvre — refusing consent (which then and now I believe to have been not legally required) — was thwarting the will of the province and city. Why? It appeared to be sour grapes because the Island residents had fought Metro and won — there was no compelling public-policy reason.

The consequences, though, were serious. The residents were required to repair their houses and were subject to prosecution, fines, and quite serious sanctions if they failed to comply with a city order — but because they could not get building permits, they were subject to prosecution if they did repair their houses — including the possibility of being ordered to remove the offending construction. It was an outrageous abuse of governmental authority. The residents were literally prosecuted if they did, and prosecuted if they didn't.

To make matters worse, media, particularly the *Toronto Star*, were not on the Islanders' side, printing the most outrageous lies about them — that they were illegal squatters (they weren't), they didn't pay taxes or rent (they did — rents offered in the arbitration were far higher than those paid by other Island tenants like the Royal Canadian Yacht Club), that the costs of city services like fire and police service on the Island were only incurred by the city because of the residents (both fire and police were necessary regardless), and many others, always done in colourful language. One article, written by a *Star* reporter who was, coincidentally, also named David Miller, was so offensive that two residents retained me to sue for defamation.

The *Star* brought a preliminary motion to dismiss the case, arguing that the residents had no claim because the comments were made about the group, not individuals. In court, I argued that my clients were identifiable members of the group that was libelled, and therefore could sue. I was successful in my precedent-setting argument: my clients were able to maintain their suit, and an out-of-court settlement was reached shortly afterward.

I was happy for them and defended the rest of the residents well. But the situation was outrageous. At one point, I appeared before a committee with some Island residents — at either City or Metro Hall, I cannot remember which — and was shocked by what I saw happen. Just before us, a wealthy resident of Forest Hill appeared, seeking significant permissions from the city, and was treated extremely well, with councillors bending backwards to ingratiate themselves with her. When my clients appeared, asking simply for the right to apply for a building permit in order to comply with a city order directing them to obtain a permit, they were insulted and ignored by committee members. I couldn't believe that these people were elected, and was determined to do something about it.

At the time, in the late 1980s, politics was very exciting in Ontario. In 1985, the Liberals and NDP had signed a historic accord, and the Liberals became the government after Lieutenant Governor Aird accepted that the Progressive Conservative minority did not have the confidence of the house, ending forty-three years of Conservative rule in Ontario. It was a time of great activism in government, with groundbreaking laws — like pay equity and the elimination of user fees for medicare — being adopted by the coalition, and such projects as great expansions to public transit were being proposed.

By this time I was a member of the NDP, gradually becoming more and more active, handing out leaflets in my Parkdale neighbourhood, knocking on doors during elections, fundraising, eventually becoming an executive member of our riding association. Something else significant was happening in my life too.

I met Jill Arthur on January 2, 1987, at a conference teaching young lawyers how to argue appeals. Jill was speaking with a woman, Christine Medland, whom I had met a few times, and I was certain Jill and I had also met. I said hello to Chris, and turned to Jill and said, "Hi, I am David Miller. Haven't we met somewhere before?"

Jill looked me right in the eyes, said "No," said goodbye to Chris, and walked off. I knew at that very moment that we would get married and have children, and although it took a while for me to get up the nerve to ask her out, I did. We dated for several years and ultimately, on June 15, 1991, we were married.

But I am getting a little ahead of myself. In the late 1980s I was getting more and more active in the NDP, and was paying more and more attention to City Hall. Other clients — like the business owners at the St. Lawrence Market — had retained me, and I had other dealings with Metro and City Hall that continually convinced me that there was a deep need for modernization and change.

I was also throwing myself more and more into the progressive side of my practice. In addition to our many corporate clients, I was acting on a legal-aid basis for refugee claimants from places like Iran and eastern Europe, hearing stories — confirmed by outside impartial evidence — of great hardship and persecution suffered by people such as Tamil families from Sri Lanka. I enjoyed this work and was so impressed by the strength and resilience of the families who came from around the world to live in Canada, in Toronto, in relative prosperity, seeking opportunity in this most liveable of cities. In addition, Jill, although Canadian, was a migrant too, having been born in Trinidad to a Venezuelan mother and Canadian father, and having grown up in countries like Venezuela, Jamaica, and Colombia; this gave me an additional perspective on those communities.

My interest in social justice and city politics came together as a result of the election of Bob Rae's NDP government on September 6, 1990. There was incredible euphoria at their election; people have forgotten, but in the next summer, despite the beginnings of the recession brought about by the first free trade agreement, in which Ontario lost hundreds of thousands of manufacturing jobs as companies that had been here for decades pulled up shop overnight and moved to the U.S., the Rae government was still at sixty per cent in the polls.

As an active member of the High Park NDP executive, and as someone who knew that our local governments badly needed progressive change, I got involved in the preparation for the 1991 municipal election. I hoped we could find candidates who could change the local political culture and fight for policies that could make our city succeed for all of its residents — not just the ones with easy access to power. I became a member of the candidate search committee, with Jane Karwat (now my chief of staff) and Jill Marzetti (my first campaign manager in the 2003 mayoral election). We interviewed possible candidates, for recommendation to the executive for its endorsement, and two were clear choices: Rosemary Martiniuk — a local social worker of Ukranian heritage, born and raised in Bloor West Village — for city councillor, and Karen Ridley — a local teacher — for public school trustee. But we could not find a candidate who was prepared to stand for Metro Council. Finally, one night after a meeting, I drove Jane home and as I dropped her off she said, "What about you? You'd make a good candidate."

The question caught me totally off-guard. Although I had avidly followed politics, and friends had joked with me at Lakefield about becoming prime minister, I had not seriously considered being a candidate. I was a partner at a prominent Bay Street law firm with an excellent practice, was well-paid (in 1994 my compensation was higher than I will ever be paid as mayor), and was about to get married.

I spoke with Jill, talked to some trusted advisors, and Mum, and spoke with Jane and Jill Marzetti again. When they both assured me that I was unlikely to win, my mind was made up: I would seek the party's endorsement and carry the flag into the 1991 municipal election, a few months after being married.

Getting the endorsement turned out to be a fight; some members of the riding association said that I couldn't possibly be a real New Democrat because I worked on Bay Street. Ultimately, the riding association endorsed me, and I set out to campaign that fall. My opponent was a wily Conservative incumbent, Derwyn Shea. It was unheard of to unseat an incumbent, but the campaign started on a note that angered me, and I forgot all about being unlikely to win.

The unofficial kickoff date for a municipal election is Labour Day. That weekend, Derwyn's household newsletter, paid for by the Metro government, arrived, yellow, like his election signs, folded cleverly so that it read, below a photo of him: "It's time to vote Derwyn Shea." Of course, when opened it said "Derywn Shea fall newsletter," but it still offended my sense of fair play that he would use public funds for blatant electoral purposes. I threw myself into the campaign, seeking a leave of absence from my firm and knocking on door after door. It also caused me to make a mistake I have not made since: I attacked Derwyn personally (rather than attacking his policies). I believe you should fight for what you believe in — colourful attacks on policies are fine, but not personal attacks. Personal attacks taint everyone involved.

Jane Karwat, my campaign manager, did something very smart; she made me canvass all of the rooming houses in Parkdale, and although I had lived at King and Jameson among and with the same people, I never realized the dire circumstances many Parkdalians lived in until I actually knocked on their doors. After one long day I said to Jane, "What is the point? None of them are going to vote." Her reply: "You are going to be representing them if you win. You'd better know who they are and what they need their government to do for them." It's a lesson I have never forgotten.

I was not successful in that election, but received nearly eight thousand votes, far more than expected. This prompted serious calls for me to run again, and I did in the 1993 federal election. It was not a good time to run as a New Democrat, and, although I did relatively well compared to other New Democrats, the incumbent Liberal, Jesse Flis, won in a landslide.

The 1994 municipal election was fast approaching and I had a decision to make: did I want to truly try to change the culture at the Metro government, or should I give up on electoral politics and stick to campaigning for others? After long discussions with Jill and Jane, I decided to run. Aird & Berlis had been generous to me, but representing legal aid clients was becoming more and more difficult at a Bay Street law firm — the billing pressures were so intense that you were almost forced to act only for the firm's business clients. Consequently, I decided that I should resign my partnership and run for office. People were stunned that I would resign to run, but I felt I had to make a total commitment, and I did. I campaigned vigorously, and under Jane's guidance, effectively, and, on November 14, 1994, was elected the new Metro councillor for High Park, defeating Tory Tony Clement and former MP Andrew Witer.

The role of city councillor is not fully appreciated, but a good one is invaluable. A good councillor is available seven days a week, understands his or her community, and knows how to work with people to build a consensus about how to move the community forward. I had the privilege my first two terms of representing Parkdale as well as High Park. I threw myself into the work and, like any good councillor, knew people on a first-name basis on every block of my ward. I also knew their issues, challenges, and hopes for their neighbourhood.

My 1994 and 1997 campaigns focused on similar issues: public transit, community policing, investment in public services and people, jobs, the environment, and fair taxes, as well as local issues like traffic calming, bike lanes, new bus service, and certain development issues.

At the first council meeting, I was appointed to the Board of Governors of Exhibition Place, thanks to timely intervention of Councillor Howard Moscoe. As part of its renewal, Exhibition Place was about to launch a competition for a new trade centre — now named the Direct Energy Centre. I was able to see first-hand how to manage an important city building project (delivered ahead of schedule, on budget), and create jobs and opportunity — all under the able leadership of Councillor Joe Pantalone. The Direct Energy Centre has met all of its projections about job creation and economic growth, and is a state of the art, beautifully designed public building.

At the same time, there was another job-creation program that had the full support of the provincial government: a proposal to extend two subway lines and build two new ones. The extensions were to be north to York University from Downsview, and west to Sherway from Kipling, and the two new lines were to be west on Eglinton from the University line to the airport, and east on Sheppard from Yonge Street. The lines became a political battle over cost, and, underlying that, the Conservatives and Liberals on council did not want to give Bob Rae a political victory. I supported all four projects: it had been far too long since we had expanded our transit system, and thousands of local, well-paid union construction jobs would be created — a needed boost for an economy still struggling to recover from the thousands of manufacturing jobs lost due to free trade. The politics dictated otherwise: North York mayor Mel Lastman put his political weight behind Sheppard (because he wanted more development at Yonge and Sheppard) and Alan Tonks, the chair of Metro Council, supported the Eglinton line, and these were the expansions that received the support of council.

Construction started quickly on Eglinton, but when the Harris government was elected later in 1995 one of their early acts was to cancel the Eglinton line (which went through the riding that Bob Rae represented provincially and Alan Tonks municipally), forcing the TTC to to spend one hundred million dollars of provincial and Metro money to dig a hole and then fill it in again. An unbelieveable waste of public money, and an incredibly shortsighted approach to city building. Needed rapid transit expansion deferred, yet again.

The province cut in other ways too. The Rae government had embarked on a program of building new schools — schools that included purpose-built childcare centres. The Harris government did not believe in childcare and refused to provide the normal subsidy to these centres. One was in Parkdale, another in North Toronto. Anne Johnston, John Godfrey (the MP for North Toronto), and I worked hard, and with the support of chair Alan Tonks and Olivia Chow, we eventually persuaded Metro to assume the provincial share of these daycares; any other result would have been unacceptable. Other city-wide issues also occupied my time, like stopping cuts to accessibility programs at the TTC, and stopping an appeal by Metro against a court order that gave two brave employees same-sex benefits.

Of course, I worked strongly on local issues, including turning an abandoned police station at 1313 Queen Street in Parkdale into a hub for artists and the local community; cleaning up the western beaches; installing bike lanes on Colborne Lodge Drive and a new bus route on Parkside Drive; working with superintendent Keith Forde of 11 Division and the local community on leading police strategies like neighbourhood patrols; and numerous community meetings on every conceivable issue, from development to traffic calming to liquor licences, and more.

I also helped to achieve something that ended a simmering controversy in Parkdale between middle-class homeowners, angry about the proliferation of illegal rooming houses, and anti-poverty activists, who saw them as the last hope for those who were the least well-off. From both canvassing and living in Parkdale, I knew the conditions that people were forced to live in, and they were unacceptable, to say the least. After numerous community meetings with city staff and my colleague, Councillor Korwin-Kuczynski, we implemented the Parkdale Pilot Project — a project that would legalize rooming houses if they met certain standards of safety, living conditions, and so forth. In essence, it meant that in some rooming houses there would be fewer, but better and safer, units. That project helped hundreds of the least well-off residents of Toronto to live in dignity.

The result of all of this was that I learned important lessons about myself, working with people, and how to succeed on an issue in local government. After being re-elected in 1997, I served as chair of the committee to oversee amalgamation, as the caucus whip for the Greater Toronto Services Board, and as a member of the TTC. I fought strongly, and effectively, for the environment, public service, and public transit. Post-amalgamation was chaotic, and I looked heavily to the example and wisdom of experienced council-lors like Anne Johnston in helping to chart a course through the politics of the Mel Lastman era, and fight the results of the massive downloading of provincial services to the city — a move that has crippled city finances to this day.

I faced a tough battle in the 2000 elections against Bill Saunder-cook. The boundaries of our ridings had been changed, and I faced the challenge of defeating Bill, who was a popular incumbent with fifteen years on city council. Politically, there was a clear difference between me and Bill: he had voted to send Toronto's garbage to a lake in Northern Ontario that was once an open-pit mine (the Adam's Mine), and I had bitterly opposed it because it risked polluting the northern waters for generations. I felt confident that the differences were clear enough that I could win, but halfway through the campaign, it mattered much less.

My mother had been having tests for some time because she had lost energy, and just did not seem right. She was a woman who had received a full payout of her sick bank because she had never missed a day of work. On a Friday afternoon I took her to the hospital where we received the news: my mother had cancer. The rest of the campaign is a blank — I won, substantially, but was absorbed by her health. Tragically, her cancer was one that had a high survivability rate if the tumour could be removed, but it was so close to her aeorta that the surgery wasn't an option. She received terrific palliative care in her apartment across the street, and Jill was magnificent, but we watched Mum wither away until she died, holding my hand — just her and me — on September 23, 2001. She showed incredible bravery and never complained about her fate, preferring to spend time with Julia and Simon — particularly Julia, to whom she would give bright shinny pennies when her granddaughter visited. I often asked Mum if she would like me to bring friends from her teaching days in Ottawa to visit, and she said, "No, I want them to remember me as I was — happy and alive." When she died we asked Julia if she wanted to come to the visitation, and she said, "No, I want to remember Nana as she was — happy and alive."

While my mother was ill, lots of people spoke to me about running for mayor. Like them, although I personally liked Mel Lastman, I couldn't abide the city government he was leading — it was run for the benefit of insiders, allowed corruption, like the MFP scandal, to flourish, and there was no plan to build a city for the twenty-first century — one that was prosperous, liveable, and had opportunity for all. These issues were all revealed by the decision to build the bridge to the Island airport — a decision that favoured the back-room interests of one well-connected businessman over the interests of thousands of jobs in waterfront revitalization, the interests of tens of thousands of Torontonians without cottages who used the Island as their park, the interests of the film industry, those of thousands of condominium residents at the waterfront, and of course, the Islanders.

It was a difficult decision, though in September 2001 Julia was six, Simon four. Already, the demands of elected office made it difficult for me to be the kind of husband or father I believed I should be, although I did have one treat as dad: walking my children to daycare and then to the local public school almost every day. Nobody needed their councillor at 8:30 a.m.

In the midst of my grief over the passing of my mother, I was approached by a constituent, prominent businessman Tom Kierans, a Conservative. Tom believed in me because he thought I could bring good government to a city that desperately needed it, supported my rumoured run for mayor, and wanted to help. At his suggestion, I met with John Laschinger, a prominent Conservative political strategist, and Patrick Gossage, a prominent Liberal media guru. I also met with the United Steelworkers and Brian Cochrane from CUPE local 416, both of whom were supportive from the start, as were city councillors Joe Pantalone, Howard Moscoe, Anne Johnston, and Sandra Bussin.

I had an important conversation with David Crombie, whose first question of me was, "If you don't run for mayor, will you run again as councillor?" As I thought about that, I realized the answer was "no." I had done what I could as a councillor. I believed Toronto needed a progressive mayor who believed in public service, and who was prepared to build a city for all residents through great services like public transit. It was clear to me that there was no candidate with that agenda, and therefore no one I could support.

With the help of this group, I began my run for mayor on January 2, 2003.

Although my campaign would be defined by the Island airport, to me, and to the Torontonians who supported me, that issue was symbolic of a city governement that was not acting in the interests of individual Torontonians. In my nine years as councillor, I had met people from every neighbourhood in this city. My opponents assumed that I only knew downtown: in fact, I knew the people, stories, and neighbourhoods across the city.

And I had another advantage — in the same way that when I met Jill I knew we would be married and have children, I knew that I was supposed to run for mayor. While victory was uncertain, I knew absolutely that I was put on earth to run. That knowledge allowed me the freedom to throw myself into the election with absolute commitment, and I worked literally sixteen hours a day every day at a grassroots level at events across Toronto.

People of course know the result: I was elected mayor of Toronto on November 10, 2003. Very few know the Toronto that I have witnessed as councillor and as mayor: a Toronto whose people are doing remarkable things, often out of the sight of the media; a Toronto where bank managers become homeless — then find their way off the street; a Toronto where selfless newcomers reach out to help others, only to be forced to overcome family tragedies; a Toronto where innovative young environmentalists are leading the world in strategies to fight climate change. That is the Toronto that is seen through my eyes.

ELIZABETH AMER

L iz Amer can boast of many political achievements in her time as the councillor of Ward 5. She was instrumental in the hiring of one of the first city department heads in decades, and in more representative hiring practices at City Hall in general. She helped establish the Harbourfront Community Centre, which provided badly needed services such as a school and daycares where there were none before. With colleague Dale Martin, she spent six years — her entire tenure in office — planning the Lillian H. Smith Public Library; the ribbon-cutting ceremony, attended by such literary figures as Dennis Lee and Michael Ondaatje, was especially satisfying. I met Liz and came to know her well when I acted for the Island residents while at Aird & Berlis in the 1980s.

But perhaps the most defining moment of Liz's political career came before she ran for office. That was when, on a July afternoon in 1980, she made a stand on Algonquin Bridge against city officials coming to evict the Toronto Islands community of Ward's and Algonquin islands. It was a day that shaped not only her own life, but that of Toronto as well.

⟜✦⟝

LIZ AMER'S HISTORY on Toronto Island goes back generations before she fought for the right to stay there. Her grandparents lived there, back when the Toronto Islands community consisted of platforms that summer visitors built for tents. When roads and year-round water sources were built, they and many others became permanent residents. Hanlan's Point got an amusement park, as well as the legendary baseball field where Babe Ruth hit his first professional home run. During the postwar housing crisis, more families arrived and built houses. The community expanded to include a movie theatre, bowling alley, stores, and dance halls.

As a child, Liz would spend her summers at her grandparents' house, just steps away from the Ward's Island Beach. It was a wholesome setting, providing the routine and ritual she needed. Every morning without fail, her grandmother would get up and do the laundry, then serve a breakfast consisting of burnt toast with margarine, canned grapefruit, and instant coffee.

She was never at a loss for things to do on the Islands. Liz was friends with most of the other children. As teenagers, they gathered in a large group on the beach to play instruments and sing songs. It was a wonderful social scene, with many inspiring young people to hang out with — a marked contrast from the working-class industrial neighbourhood in which she spent the rest of the year.

As an adult, Liz eventually bought her own house on Ward's Island in order to stay close to her childhood paradise.

For the Island, everything changed in 1954. A new regional government, the Municipality of Metropolitan Toronto Council, was established to build the infrastructure necessary for a growing city, such as sewers, transportation, police stations, and parks. The regional government — better known as Metro — assumed control of the Toronto Islands, and its parks commissioner, Tommy Thompson, decided that the islands were a park and therefore not zoned for residential housing. The Toronto Islands community, which, at its peak in the fifties, consisted of around 630 cottages and homes, was marked for removal. Hanlan's Point, Centre Island, and the other communities were removed — sometimes the home-owners would float their houses to Ward's and Algonquin islands to begin anew.

By 1980, council began the final action to evict the homeowners of Ward's and Algonquin islands. The residents of those islands had chosen to fight to stay, and had been actively organizing for years, fighting politically at every level of government. In fact, the City of Toronto supported the Islanders, arguing that the small residential community made the Islands safer and more interesting. Metro, how-ever, pressed on, insisting that every single house must go.

That summer, the Toronto Island community received an inside tip that the city was planning to send notices of eviction to every-one on the Islands. Alarmed, groups of people were quickly organized into "squadrons" and tasked with specific jobs in an effort to counter any eviction campaign mounted from the mainland. They even went so far as to stage rehearsals on the Islands with a troupe of actors — partly to prepare everyone for the real thing, and partly to show the government that they were willing to fight to protect their homes.

Liz invited activists from the People or Planes movement — the group that successfully organized to fight the proposed Pickering Airport — to speak at a meeting she had organized. The three women — Anne Howes, Frances Moore, and Brenda Davies — had helped prevent the building of the airport in the Cedarwood community of Pickering Township by hunkering down in an abandoned farmhouse on the proposed site, defying government officials and bulldozers alike. It was inspiring to hear them talk about their experience, and to realize that anything was possible.

People were still scared, however, so for the next night's meeting, "The Game" was organized. Everyone was told to bring something precious — something they could not afford to lose. They were then divided into two teams, with each team's goal to acquire the other's treasures. The Game lasted all afternoon, and was successful in showing people not just what the stakes were, but also how determined they could be when put in a position to lose something they love.

On the morning of July 28, their mole in the attorney general's office sent an alert: the sheriff was moving in that day. Metro sent a garbage truck down to the community to gather intelligence, but did not spot their lookouts, so when the sheriff began moving cars from the island airport at three p.m., everyone was ready to take action. The air raid sirens that had been set up for just that occasion went off. People who were on the mainland at the time were called back to the site; among them was Linda Rosenbaum from *This* magazine, who had taken a cab to get down to the lake in time, and whose cabbie decided to stay and help her defend her home. They were to travel to the foot of York Street, where the Islanders' "navy" — a fleet consisting of private boats — was assembled to ferry everyone back to their cottages. By the time all was said and done, about two thousand people were ready to go.

The plan was to gather at Algonquin Bridge, the narrowest point

of entry to Algonquin Island, where they would link arms and form a blockade. For the benefit of the media, the people at the front held a banner that said "Save us Bill Davis" — a plea to the premier of Ontario. When the sheriff arrived and introduced himself, Liz knew the only thing to do was to confront him. She stepped onto the bridge to plead her case, arguing that the writs of execution written up by the Metro Council were out of date. She pleaded successfully for a twenty-four-hour grace period, while the judge deliberated. When the sheriff and his deputy turned to leave, the crowd went wild.

The events of that day paved the way for provincial legislation to protect the Ward's Island community. On December 15, 1993, Rae's government passed Bill 61, giving every member of the community ninety-nine-year leases, which were paid for in cash two years later. Because the arrangement is between the community and the province, it is now very difficult for any resident to lose their land without having the case examined by a provincial judge.

Liz eventually entered politics with the encouragement of Jack Layton and Dale Martin. As a member of the NDP, she was elected councillor for Ward 5, representing the central waterfront communities, the business district, Chinatown, and the University of Toronto. Her two terms — the first in 1988, the second in 1991 — took place during an NDP golden age, when the party represented the majority of the city's executive jobs and standing committees; it made it much easier for Liz to use the activist experience she had gained on Ward's Island to enact change. It is for this reason that she does not like to take personal credit for any of her political achievements: she sees them as the result of teamwork.

Liz still lives on Ward's Island. Though she has resided there alone for about twenty years, she never feels lonely. There is something about being completely surrounded by water that turns neighbours into kindred spirits — things like having to rely on each other for even simple necessities like toilet paper can really unite a community. She knows that, when the chips are down, she can count on her neighbours, and they can count on her. It is thanks to this solidarity that the communities on Ward's and Algonquin islands still stand.

ANNE JOHNSTON

Anne Johnston understands her life as a series of events extending from one vivid and early childhood experience. She was seven years old the night the lights went out across Britain and she can remember being with her family in a place called Llandudno. Their home in south Wales was being bombed because the Anglo-Iranian Oil Company was based in the region and was an enemy target. She recalls being taken on a walk by her parents that night to Conwy Castle to see the lights on the beautiful bridge that led across the moat. As they came up over the ridge road the beautiful castle stood before her, its lights glowing magically.

Her memory of that night is vivid. She can even tell you what she was wearing — white socks with ducks around them, little black shoes, and a hand-knitted coat her mother had made her from blue wool. Strange that the memory is so idyllic when the

sojourn was to stand and wait for the magical lights to extin-
guish, an ominous signal that the world was now at war and her
only comfort was her parents' warm hands holding hers. She felt
very grown-up that night. It was a signal from her parents that
she was old enough to witness history in the making (her younger
sister had been left behind with an aunt). Such acute memories
of childhood are rare, she thinks, but seventy years later she
knows precisely how each moment shaped her future.

I know how Anne shaped my future, and that of the City of
Toronto. First elected as a city councillor in the reform movement
of 1972, Anne served Toronto and its people with great distinction for more than thirty years. Never afraid to take on entrenched
interests, Anne is responsible for great advances in public health
and equity, particularly for women and the disabled. Things we
take for granted now — like protection from lead poisoning and
accessibility to public buildings, not to mention the role of women
in politics — are due in part to Anne Johnston's principled, non-
partisan, and effective advocacy. Even in her last term as a city
councillor, she was fighting to clean up the evident corruption at
City Hall, and was the councillor who both proposed and moved
the motion to create the MFP inquiry. The Anne Johnston Health
Station is a fitting tribute to her, as was the national award she
received in 2010 from the Federation of Canadian Municipalities. In fact, as I write this book, Anne is leading the charge to
stop the installation of wind turbines in her beloved Pontypool.
(We may disagree on this item, but I certainly won't fight her!)

I knew of Anne Johnston, of course, before I knew her personally
— she was already a legend in Toronto political circles — but

two events caused me to be very close to her. We first met after I was elected councillor in 1994. My daughter Julia was born the following August, and when she was about a year old, I brought her to council and placed her on my seat. Anne was in the Chair at the time, and said, with a hint of the Welsh lilt that remains in her voice, "There is a stranger in the house" (which means someone unelected is on the floor of council). Julia heard this, and whether it was Anne's voice or appearance, I do not know, but she yelled "Nana" at the top of her lungs as only a one-year-old can! She'd mistaken Anne for my mum, Joan. The chamber burst into laughter, and at that moment Anne and I bonded.

The second event that drew me close to Anne was a happy coincidence. After amalgamation, Anne and I were seated together on the new city council, and she acted as a wise advisor — perhaps an aunt — from then on.

BORN IN 1932 in the town of Swansea, Anne's early years were entirely about family togetherness. Her life was filled with arts and literature, and many activities. She remembers being introduced by her father to a strange local man who used to come around: he wore corduroy pants and a turtleneck sweater and would write poems on shoeboxes in her gran's attic. Her father once said, "And do you know who this man is, Anne?" To which she replied, "Yes — gentle Jesus." It wasn't until years later that she learned to use his real name, "Dylan Thomas," and understood that the words on those boxes belonged to something called *Under Milk Wood*. Thomas was her cousin's godfather.

Anne may have thought of Thomas as "gentle Jesus," but some of her relatives thought he was a reprobate who spent too much time in the pub. Anne's family never went to a pub themselves, and by the time she was in her teens Anne was convinced she was preparing herself for Wimbledon. But that aspect of her early life has worn off — she doesn't mind a decent whisky now.

Anne's mother was in the Women's Voluntary Service and played a key role in evacuating families like theirs during the Blitz. Her father was part of the Home Guard and a head teacher at a local school in Swansea, where he was involved in theatre arts. Together the family started a theatre in town. Anne had been a hit on stage as a baby; she'd apparently been very good — she hadn't cried or made a fuss, she was told. She believes that spending her early years with theatre around her meant she was never afraid to talk or debate in groups or in front of an audience.

Much of Anne's time as she grew up was spent focused on tennis. She was good. She remembers she and her partner created quite a stir by beating a team from the boys' school. When she was sixteen she was scouted by Fred Perry, who was looking for juniors to develop for Wimbledon. She's convinced she would have made it had she not just missed the age cut-off.

She passed her high school certificate and was accepted at Cardiff University for medicine and Oxford University and the University of London for occupational therapy. The emphasis in those days was not on choosing a career; rather, it was on having a job to support yourself in case your husband died. Mothers of her generation carried the belief that you had to support your children — you didn't think about yourself.

She chose London over Cardiff and began working with a doctor in the field of community psychiatry.

It was at this time in her life that she fell in love with an American Jewish psychoanalyst, Dr. Robert Corday. But when his family objected to her not being Jewish, the relationship dissolved. She was devastated, but through Corday she had been introduced to the practice of psychoanalysis and the power of Freud's ideas on projection. They were incredibly informative years in London, and she'd socialized with some of the key figures in the European psychoanalytic movement, which included Freud's daughter Anna, and Princess Marie Bonaparte. She eventually published a paper on "The Study of Projective Techniques" in which she examined painting and pottery as therapeutic methods.

But with no obvious career ahead of her in England, Anne boarded a ship late in the autumn of 1955 and set sail for Montreal. She arrived on November 11 — "Armistice Day," as it was known then. She had twenty-five quid in her pocket and was frozen to the bone in a long white coat. While on the ship she met another occupational therapist and together they set up in Montreal.

Soon, Anne met a Scotsman, whom she married a year later. Her working life was put on hold as the couple began to raise a family. After a move to Toronto and ten years as a stay-at-home mother, she had a burning desire to engage her head again and went back to work at the Queen Street Mental Health Centre. It soon became clear to her that she was facing real sexism in that part-time job. She was also aware that she and another female colleague weren't getting the benefits the male workers were getting. On her fortieth birthday, she made a vow that she was never going to hear another racist or sexist remark without objecting to it.

Her consciousness was being raised, and the period from 1968 to 1972 would lead her straight to City Hall — and eventually, as

chair of the personnel committee, she would oversee an "equal pay for work of equal value" policy that ensured male public health inspectors were no longer being paid more than female public health nurses (who in some cases had more qualifications, but were paid less because of their gender).

She soon discovered that her background in occupational therapy, group dynamics, and "projective techniques" had very direct applications for dealing in politics. She became addicted to City Hall at a time when Spadina was the big issue, John Sewell was the big star, and David Crombie was alderman. It was during a Committee of Adjustment process that Anne stood up and challenged Crombie about a high-rise development at 500 Duplex Avenue. On hearing the bite of her fading Welsh accent and the booming voice projection she'd developed in her theatre days, Crombie was so surprised that his only response was, "Where have you been all my life?"

The Welsh are known as little people who love to fight, but Anne will also tell you they are little people with voices, and they love to sing. Everybody has a voice in Wales; nobody will dare tell someone they don't have a voice. But until the Crombie moment she didn't know she had a *political* voice.

Despite her successes, Anne was still seeing that the world wasn't shaped for women — it was shaped for men. She remembers being appalled at how the washrooms at City Hall disproportionately catered to the men: there were no dedicated women's washrooms. She had that changed.

In the 1972 municipal election, David Crombie was originally running for senior alderman and Anne Johnston had decided to run for junior alderman. But after Crombie decided to run for mayor, Anne ran for alderman and faced heavy competition from Larry Grossman and David Smith. Anne beat them both. She won

16,555 votes in her first election and became the only woman on council.

The reform council of 1972 was the youngest council in Canada; they were all in their forties under Crombie. Politics for Anne was always about trying to involve everyone. One of Anne's strong beliefs was that the best way to do this at council was not to have party politics, but to try to work to common goals. She felt this was better than having an NDP group, a Liberal group, and a Tory group. While she herself would most often vote along the same lines as the NDP, she resisted becoming too tightly tied to the party, which she felt could be, at times, too "doctrinaire." But by and large, she saw the NDP and Liberals pitted against what she calls "the dinosaurs."

For thirty-one years Anne worked as a municipal councillor, with a three-year break from 1985 to 1988 after running for and losing the mayoralty election against Art Eggleton.

Anne was probably the first person to openly campaign for the chair of the Board of Health. Among the accomplishments of the board under her leadership was a conference they hosted on Healthy Cities as a contribution to the 150th anniversary of Toronto. The conference attracted delegates from around the world and marked the birth of the worldwide Healthy Cities movement.

There are countless other examples of Anne's leadership — which always involved engaging the community. She chaired both the Mayor's Committee on the Disabled and the Elderly and the Metro Council committee that established Wheel-Trans. Both involved extensive public engagement, and had a profound positive impact on the ability of people to live in an accessible city.

One of the real fights of her career emerged around the issue of lead poisoning. In the seventies and eighties she sat as chair of the Board of Health and was sued for bias, as was the whole board.

There were two lead smelters in Toronto that emitted particulate matter the board maintained was hazardous to the health of nearby residents, the children playing in their gardens and schoolyards, and the workers in the plants. After conducting an epidemiological study, the board, under Anne's direction, adopted the criteria for lead in the air that they had been recommending to the province. That's when the battle commenced. The fight went on for years and years, and in the end the province finally adjusted their air-quality criteria and brought it down to the level the city had adopted. But the smelters accused them of being biased. When her lawyer asked her if she was, she remembers saying, "Yes, I'm biased in support of peoples' health." Ultimately, Anne and the board won the suit.

POLITICS IS ALWAYS about truly engaging residents and allowing them to shape the city they want. Anne will tell you, "The process is the most important thing in the lot." An emblem of Anne's fight for process can be seen every March 1 when City Hall flies a strange flag with a pink dragon on a white and green background. It's the Welsh flag for St. David's Day, and Anne Johnston is the one who fought for it to be flown annually.

Today Anne describes herself as even more fierce than she used to be — a trait that probably comes with age. There's a sense that time is running out and there are still things she wants to see happen.

Anne feels people have lost the technique for practising politics. She remembers fighting market value assessments and attending a meeting at the Royal York Hotel. She got up on the platform but wasn't yet sure what she was going to say. Quickly, however, a slogan and a song came to her. She said, "I just don't think there's another word to say except 'no way' — 'no way MVA.'" Her chant turned the room into a full-tilt rally.

Now one of her main concerns is ageism. She doesn't like being told what to do because of her age. She still feels about forty, just as good in her head, just as capable of coming up with a rational reason for doing something ... though getting in and out of the car is a bloody chore, and "walking to the john" is a real hassle. She doesn't believe she's that ancient, even though her daughter recently took her for an Alzheimer's test. She passed with flying colours but was annoyed as heck with her daughter, she says, laughing.

Despite any mock annoyance, Anne is delighted to see her daughters have taken on some of her traits. This is likely because she brought her kids up to be self-sufficient. She describes having a credit system on the fridge that included points for doing jobs, laundry, and the dishwasher. At the end of the week the kids would add up the points. Anne found that by age twelve they could do their own washing; "They'd grown up." The system was so successful it was written up in *Homemakers* magazine.

Anne Johnston. Sexism, health, development, corruption, accessibility, and now ageism and windmills. Still fighting. Still succeeding. Every March 1 when the Welsh flag flies at City Hall, it symbolizes to me a strong, independent voice that never gives up. Yes, that describes Wales — but it also describes my friend Anne.

LAURA REINSBOROUGH

Most of us, when we look at Toronto, see concrete and glass, pavement, brick, and stone; we see offices and houses and apartment buildings. When Laura Reinsborough moved here from Sackville, New Brunswick, she saw the ravines and parks, and especially the gardens. She saw an urban farm. Since 2003, she has been working steadily to make her vision a reality — not just a reality for herself, but one that has benefits for many people. Her goal is to turn Toronto into an orchard.

With a number of friends and like-minded people, Laura founded Not Far from the Tree, an organization that now has 150 volunteers all over the city, picking fruit that is then given both fresh and preserved to food banks. How Laura came to found Not Far from the Tree is a journey worth following.

SACKVILLE, NEW BRUNSWICK, located on the border with Nova Scotia, halfway between the Bay of Fundy and Silver Lake, is known best for Mount Allison University. Laura's father, who taught chemistry at Mount Allison, studied to be a Catholic priest with the Basilian Order. From him she learned that science and spirituality in all their forms coexist in the act of gardening. Laura's childhood experience was largely rural: in summer she and her friends canoed and played "sink the dock" — a game where she, the youngest child in the crowd, invariably found herself at the sinking end of the dock. In winter, Silver Lake became an ice rink that she skated and played hockey on. Her father maintained a garden in the backyard of the family home, and the vegetables he grew in the yard were the main focus of his attention in the summer months. One year, when she was old enough, her father gave Laura a patch of her own to grow green peppers. From that moment on, she has enjoyed gardening deeply and to this day the green pepper is her favourite vegetable. The growing part of a garden is not all Laura remembers. She recalls pulling up carrots, digging potatoes, picking beans and shelling them. The trip from the backyard garden to the kitchen table is one she made many, many times.

After receiving her undergraduate degree from Mount Allison, Laura decided that she wanted to pursue a master's degree in environmental studies. She chose to attend York University, where she read the influential books of Rachel Carson and Henry David Thoreau. These works frustrated her because they espoused a separation between urban centres and rural areas that she had not experienced. It was her reaction to these books in particular, as well as an awareness of the increasing urbanization of the world and the urban sprawl of Toronto, that fuelled Laura's resolve to learn more about the wilderness and gardens and orchards contained within city limits. Her passion led her to work towards a single goal: to find a way to live in a sustainable manner in a large city, the city she had adopted — Toronto.

Soon after starting in the graduate program in environmental studies at York, she discovered that a group of professors at UCLA had turned fruit harvesting into a form of public theatre. These professors would dress up in sanitation suits to undertake their clandestine actions, and under cover of night would descend upon various neighbourhoods to pick fruit and fill shopping carts with it. While these activities might sound illegal, they are not: the branches of any fruit-bearing tree that overhang public property are considered "public fruit." This law is rooted in an ancient Roman law, *Usufruct*. This statute decreed that any person had the right to benefit from someone else's property if that property was not damaged in the process.

Laura was enchanted by the story of the UCLA group and the impact they made by calling attention to this old practice. She was particularly struck by the power a group of people could have when they gathered around a cause.

While completing her studies at York she decided to volunteer at a local famer's market in her neighborhood of St. Paul's in Ward 21. The market took place on Saturdays and was pretty ad hoc; Laura was happy to be an extra pair of helping hands and would set up tables and chairs at the location, which was just a local church's front lawn. She came up with her idea one Saturday while talking with the woman who ran the market. Recounting her amazement over the Usufruct law and the idea of "public gleaning" of fruit, the market's manager pointed out that the Spadina Museum was one location in the city that had an abundance of apple trees, including a variety of heirloom species, and she wasn't sure what they were doing with the fruit.

Laura made contact with the people at the Spadina Museum to

set up her next project. The museum — former home of James Austin, founder of the Dominion Bank and president of Consumers Gas — has an orchard on its property. Someone suggested that she pick the apples, which is what she did. Picking apples is not as easy as it seems — it's hard work, and as Laura learned, there are tricks to it. When picking an apple, she discovered that she should not pull the fruit down from the branch; it's best to lift the apple up and twist until the stem snaps. She took the apples she picked to her local market, just a kilometre away.

Picking apples in the Spadina House orchard acquainted Laura with the variety of apples growing in Toronto. There were Northern Spys and Maiden Blush, as well as Bottle Greening and Northern Greening; these are firm, tart varieties best for baking, because their mealy texture makes excellent pies. The experience proved to be therapeutic for Laura, and also showed her that there was a lot of edible fruit available for picking. She remembers the apples didn't look anything like the commercial varieties we get in our supermarkets. These ones had character; they were pockmarked with scabs and they often had bugs. It made her think this was what real apples should look like, and then she tasted one and found the flavours were out of this world. She started selling the apples on the local church lawn on weekends, and quickly turned that activity into a showcase for the quality of locally grown food. Soon, the people who bought apples from her began to tell her about the fruit trees on their streets, in their neighbourhoods, including a group of Italian men who had grafted several varieties of plums onto their plum trees, so that one tree would grow five different kinds of plums.

One of Laura's great discoveries at this time took place in her own neighbourhood, which had a long history of Italian and Portuguese immigrants. Until then, Laura had only eaten dried apricots, having never seen a fresh one. She had always believed that apricots were the kind of fruit that grew better in a warmer, more southern climate — yet here in her own backyard were trees overflowing with them.

Laura began to explore more and more neighbourhoods in the city, picking the fruit that was available. The residents who saw her came out to talk to her and many of them showed her the baskets of fruit they had collected from their own trees. She realized that these streets had their own closed economies, ones where the neighbours were selling, sharing, and trading baskets of fruit. Learning about these situations, Laura began to think that it might be possible for the entire city to behave like these neighbourhoods. She also recognized the irony of Torontonians driving past local cherry trees to get to the grocery stores to buy cherries from Niagara, B.C., or California.

The next winter, Laura became convinced that the possibility she had pondered could and would become a reality. Based on her studies, experience, and knowledge of the soil in Toronto, she calculated that fruit trees in Toronto yielded more than 1.5 million pounds of fruit each year. In January of 2008, Laura and friends developed a plan for this local fruit, and called it Not Far from the Tree. They organized themselves, borrowed ladders and other necessary equipment, such as boots and gloves, and set out to pick fruit. By the end of that summer, Not Far from the Tree numbered 150 volunteers who together picked over three thousand pounds of fruit in the neighbourhoods of Ward 21.

Although the summer was a huge success, Laura felt burned out, and had to cut the picking season short, leaving fruit unpicked and wasted. She realized that in order to make Not Far from the Tree more successful, she would need some funding to support its work, which she received from the city. While she was working on her proposals and plans, the idea of eating local food to lower

greenhouse gas emissions — known as the one-hundred-kilometre diet — started to gain the public's awareness. She thought this was a great idea, and realized that her movement was itself something close to a one-kilometre version of the diet.

The following summer, 2009, the 150-volunteer organization had grown to four hundred and expanded its efforts to cover more neighbourhoods in more wards. They picked eight thousand pounds of fruit in total. As awareness of Not Far from the Tree grew, more and more people told Laura of trees in their neighbourhoods. Torontonians who knew about the organization were getting its point; the people in the city were ready, the time had arrived.

One thing that began to concern Laura, however, was that many of the people she was talking to had lost touch with the knowledge of where the food on our tables comes from, where it is grown, and where it could be grown. Even the preservation of fruit seemed to have become a cultural memory at best; few people knew how to make jams and jellies and pickles. But though they did not know how to do these things, Laura found that most people wanted to learn. She began to run preserving workshops, in which she demonstrated how to pickle beets and tomatoes, and how to make strawberry jam and cherry preserves. Though she was no longer in her mother's kitchen in Sackville — working instead on the twentieth floor of a condominium, with her hair pulled back out of her face and a white cotton apron covering her clothes — the feeling in Toronto was the same as the one she had experienced at her childhood home.

All the food harvested and preserved by Not Far from the Tree is given away; there's no monetary exchange. The people who pick and preserve are volunteers — not just with their time, but also their fruit. It's a win-win-win scenario, but the business of being a not-for-profit requires a lot of work to raise funds. Transforming it into a financially sustainable operation remains a challenge for Laura, but it is one that she does not find daunting.

Laura finds deep satisfaction in what she sees as the potential for cultural impact of her efforts. It is of deep concern to her that the average age of Ontario's farmers is now fifty-three, which means that the new generations are no longer becoming farmers. In 2009, the last canning facility in Canada shut down in the Niagara fruit-growing belt. As a result, hundreds of acres of canning-peach trees were pulled from their soil. She worries that many of our practices in food production are not sustainable, and that the global food system is threatening local production. Laura hopes that activities that have been traditionally perceived as rural ones — including the shared-work aspects of harvesting — will begin to be attractive to the residents of Toronto. She knows that eighty per cent of the soil in Toronto is Class One, which means the city is prime agricultural land; it is her hope that all available land will be put to agricultural use and that the city will not permit the removal of fruit-bearing trees. She sees a city, not too different from the Toronto of today, where plenty of fruit and vegetables are grown, and that this abundance will be shared amongst the city's population, especially with the people who turn to the city's food banks and shelters. She realizes that the ultimate goal of her project is one that addresses the gap between rich and poor.

Although she now lives a thousand miles from her childhood home, Laura retains many of the qualities instilled by her parents and the environment in which she grew up. She attributes the philanthropic aspect of her gardening to her father's background as a priest and the lessons that he and her mother taught her. But the achievement and successes of Not Far from the Tree and her efforts have not satisfied her completely; her horizons stretch far

beyond Toronto's city limits. There's one idea that enchants her —
one that she hopes to make a reality. The idea arose one night
in 2008 when she and her friends were brainstorming around
her kitchen table. Someone mentioned that a lot of fruit trees have
been growing along Canada's rail lines, the result of produce spilling
out of train cars. Laura sees a fruit orchard extending across the
country, from one coast to another, and she imagines a train car
that travels the rails, filled with volunteer fruit-pickers. Knowing
Laura, there isn't much doubt that she will make it happen.

BRAINERD BLYDEN-TAYLOR

Brainerd Blyden-Taylor is the musical director of the Nathaniel Dett Chorale, one of Canada's most accomplished professional choral ensembles. Under his leadership, the group has brought together talented singers from many different African-Canadian communities to perform for audiences ranging from high schools to American presidents. Some of what Brainerd has accomplished with the Nathaniel Dett Chorale can be traced to his forty-plus years of church music experience. But it is his work with the Toronto arts community that has taught him music can be about more than just performance — it can be a calling to something greater.

=◆=

BRAINERD'S MUSICAL STORY begins in Trinidad, where his father was a pastor at the city church in Port of Spain. In addition to his ministry, Brainerd's father had a musical background, having minored in voice and choral conducting while attending seminary school in Cincinnati. After serving as the first indigenous Wesleyan Methodist bishop of Trinidad and then bishop of the Caribbean, his father moved the family to Barbados in order to teach singers there the art of the tenor voice. It was from him that Brainerd became aware of the transformative power of choral ensembles. Not unlike playing a solo instrument, participation in a choir or orchestra requires discipline and work ethic, but, unlike playing a solo instrument, singing in a choir requires teamwork. The study of choral music teaches people how to get along with each other.

On New Year's Day, 1973, Brainerd left the Caribbean to take a position as youth leader and music director at Oakwood Wesleyan Methodist Church in Toronto's west end. He found that communities in Toronto were deeply segregated. His own congregation was almost entirely Black, while an identically named church at the other end of the city was almost entirely white. In an attempt to bring the different communities together, he and his cousins formed a gospel group called The Shepherd's Flock, which included the white son of a pastor from the east end church.

Brainerd's work with the gospel group led to a greater involvement in classical music, and his career quickly moved from strength to strength. His first big break came in 1980 when he won a classical conducting competition. The win signalled a slight change in the direction of his career. After studying with John Washburn and the Vancouver Chamber Choir, he went through the orchestral training program at the Royal Conservatory of Music and earned a licence to work as a classical conductor. His services were so in demand that he was offered the position of music director at

St. Paul's Anglican on Bloor Street — despite the fact that he is not Anglican, but Wesleyan Methodist. Other jobs he accepted included assistant conductor of the Hart House Chorus at the University of Toronto, and artistic director of the Orpheus Choir of Toronto.

Mary Lou Fallis, a board member of the Toronto Arts Council and co-chair of the music committee, watched with interest as Brainerd's star rose. She chose him to sit on the TAC music committee, citing his talent as well as the fact that he is of Caribbean descent. The TAC wanted his help in reaching out to the Black community in Toronto. Brainerd recalls explaining to them that the issue was more complicated than they thought: what they had been calling "the Black community" was actually an artificial grouping of several completely separate communities. The only relevant thing the disparate groups had in common was a love of music.

His work on the committee led Brainerd to an epiphany. According to his research, none of the professional chamber choirs across the country were performing music from the African tradition. His idea, to assemble a professional chorale that combined classically trained artists with jazz artists from various musical backgrounds, was tremendously appealing. Fallis suggested he make it happen.

The original plan was to use a small grant awarded by the Ontario Arts Council to launch Brainerd's concept at the Selafi Festival and then travel to key cities across the country auditioning singers. Unfortunately, because Brainerd had trouble convincing people that the plan could come together, he eventually returned the grant money. He realized that he needed more resources to keep the group together past the initial event, so he turned to the Canada Council for the Arts to ask for a significantly larger grant. They offered Brainerd only half the amount he had requested in autumn of 1997, but Brainerd decided it was enough to work with and accepted.

The concept was presented to the press and the public on February 24 — Fat Tuesday, also known as Mardi Gras — of the next year, barely a week after Brainerd received his articles of incorporation. He wanted to strike while the iron was hot, and later that spring, he, along with accompanist Andrew Craig and a friend from university, international opera star Measha Brueggergosman, began travelling across the country to audition for the ensemble.

Brainerd wanted to name his new chorale something that would honour both Canadian and Black music history. He briefly considered the Sheldon Brooks Singers, after the Black Ontario composer; unfortunately, Brooks did not quite fit, having not done much choral music in his career. It was at this point that Brainerd discovered a book titled *Follow Me: The Life and Music of Nathaniel Dett*, about an early twentieth-century composer from Niagara Falls, Ontario, who taught traditional music at historically Black colleges in the southern United States and, upon meeting people who had experienced slavery, was inspired to incorporate spiritual music into his compositions. Nathaniel Dett struck Brainerd as the perfect model for many reasons: the way he worked with his students, his defiance of discrimination, his thoughts on spirituality, and the groundbreaking nature of his music all reflected what the project was about. Brainerd christened his ensemble the Nathaniel Dett Chorale partly in hopes of getting Canadians to become more familiar with Dett's legacy. In honour of their namesake, the chorale's first public performance took place in Dett's hometown of Niagara Falls, in the same high school auditorium he had played in 1900.

It was not long before the Nathaniel Dett Chorale graduated from high school auditoriums to national stages. The next few years were dedicated to touring, as well as entering — and winning — competitions. But the biggest opportunity came in 2007 when Brainerd was in Virginia working on the musical staff of Hampton

University's ministers' conference. He found himself sitting on stage directly behind presidential candidate Barack Obama. Obama, who was only supposed to give a ten-minute greeting, instead delivered an hour-long speech. Brainerd was enthralled; he found the speech so arresting that he considers the experience of meeting Obama in person afterwards secondary in comparison. He saw the Democratic candidate as authentic and intriguing, and began to follow his journey to the White House.

In late 2008, when it appeared that Obama was poised to win the U.S. presidential election, Brainerd's booking agent in Montreal — an American expatriate — phoned the Canadian embassy in Washington and suggested that the Nathaniel Dett Chorale would be a perfect addition to any planned inauguration festivities. Brainerd remembers that the suggestion bounced back and forth among Toronto, Montreal, and Washington so many times that he began to doubt it would ever lead to anything. But in early December, the Canadian embassy sent word to the chorale, inviting them to the inauguration to serve as the entertainment for all embassy events.

The Nathaniel Dett Chorale was the only Canadian act to perform at the inauguration, and they represented the country admirably. They performed so well that the Smithsonian Institution invited them to perform at their event too. And when President Obama called in his speech for everyone to perform acts of service in the city during the inauguration events, the chorale took his words to heart, singing at a community centre in the inner-city community of Columbia Heights. Their final performance in Washington took place on the steps of the Canadian embassy as President Obama's parade went by.

=⟨⟩=

BRAINERD'S WORK WITH the Nathaniel Dett Chorale exemplifies everything he feels music should be about. His job has become more than one of creative direction; he has social, cultural, and political responsibilities now. The chorale he has brought together represents what Toronto is about — not just in the diversity of its influences and members, but also in the diversity of its audience. Brainerd knows he can look out at his crowd and see people of all ages and from all cultures. That, to him, is what Toronto really looks like — what it is supposed to be.

JOHN MORTON

The Student School, one of Toronto's only alternative high schools, is an institution remarkable for its focus on empathy and social justice. It has a reputation as one of the safest schools in the Toronto school system, and has helped change the lives of countless students. If anyone is responsible for helping the Student School become what it is today, it is John Morton — although he will never admit it. The twenty-five years he has spent running the school have created an environment where students feel respected and are confident that they can participate without fear of reproach. How John managed this was relatively simple: he remembered what it was like to be a student.

⟨✦⟩

JOHN GREW UP in the 1950s on Clinton Street, near Bloor and Bathurst. His neighbourhood was a diverse one; he does not remember another Anglo-Saxon family on the street aside from his. Three doors down lived the Mirvishes; as a child, he would sometimes wander to their home, where Ed's mother would feed him. His family rented out rooms to cover their own rent. Because of this — as well as the nature of his neighbourhood — John was exposed to many different kinds of people from an early age. He looks back fondly on his time on Clinton Street, and wishes the family stayed there instead of relocating to the suburbs.

The reason for the move was that John's father needed to be closer to his job at de Havilland. His role at work was changing: having proved extremely popular with the workers, he had been voted union president. The senior Morton was a man filled with tremendous empathy. He never saw himself as anything but a worker, and felt a sense of unity with the union members. John remembers being taken to union events, and listening with interest to the talk on prominent issues, as well as criticisms of management. These discussions formed the basis of his earliest political lessons.

John's other place of learning — school — was not nearly so welcoming. From the very beginning, he was considered a problem student who had trouble following school rules. At the age of four, he decided to leave during lunch hour and ended up wandering all the way home. In the fourth grade, he was kicked out of school. The administrator claimed he was too disruptive — a charge John disputes. He did not run around the classroom shouting or getting into fights. What he did do was wisecrack and ask a lot of questions — things he learned some teachers didn't appreciate, to the point where they no longer wanted him in their classes.

John was transferred to a Catholic school for grade five, but the situation only got worse. Because he was outspoken and always

ready to question what his teachers said, John was subjected to corporal punishment. Within a month of arriving, his teacher had developed a routine where she would give him the strap every morning before nine o'clock, just to keep him in line for the rest of the day.

The next year, however, was a revelation. John's new teacher was young, and dealt with him in a completely different way. For one, her sense of humour reflected his, and she actually appreciated some of his wisecracks. She still yelled at him from time to time, but because the atmosphere in her class was much more humane — and challenging — John began to respond as a student.

That he was bright was never in doubt. John once scored extremely high on an aptitude test for English and math. He remembers the day the results came in: the principal came and smacked him in the head for not performing to the level of his test scores. Needless to say, he did not respond well to that type of approach. John began to act out in a campaign of small acts of civil disobedience inspired in part by his father's independent spirit.

For the rest of elementary, and moving on into high school at Western Collegiate, John's attitude — as well as his teachers' reactions to it — resulted in poor marks. He was forced to repeat grade eleven, then failed grade twelve and decided to work in the Eaton's warehouse for a year. It wasn't until grade thirteen that things changed. As before, the change was inspired by a teacher, Donny Schmidt. Schmidt was new to the staff and the best instructor John had ever had.

He was a few credits short of earning his diploma, but Carleton University allowed him to take two night courses on a probationary basis. Unfortunately, he couldn't afford to stay in Ottawa. He returned to Toronto and applied for sociology at York University, which turned out to be an ideal learning environment for John. Free to express his opinions without fear of having a metre stick broken over his shoulders, he excelled. His grades were good enough to get him into law school or teachers' college. He chose the latter, finished the course easily, and quickly landed a teaching job.

Having been a problem student himself, John had been exposed to many different teachers' disciplinary styles. He came to several conclusions about what made teachers effective and what didn't. The first and most important conclusion was that the teacher must actually know their subject area. Beyond that, they must treat their students with humanity and respect. John's approach was to recognize that teenagers are worthy and important people with much to give. As long as he was fair and consistent, the students did not have a problem with him penalizing their peers who did wrong; and as long as they respected and listened to each other, he would allow them their say and the opportunity to object or to ask questions. John's teaching style resonated with his students, and he soon became known as someone they could talk to.

In 1981, John learned he was being transferred to the Student School. While it was officially a promotion, some of his colleagues insisted he was being sent away because the principal did not like his teaching style. John was fine with it either way; he had already accepted that his ambition to be a great and transformative teacher could not be realized in the more traditional teaching environment.

When he first arrived at the Student School, there were only about sixty students and seven teachers, but it had begun to expand rapidly as parents discovered it through word of mouth. The Student School was a place of professional opportunity; although the fundamentals of the school were in place, the overall vision and direction were still being determined. Within five years, John was steering the ship as its principal.

When a new student registers at the Student School, they are given a tour. Often, when he was principal, it was John himself who took them to see the facilities. John made it a point during the tour to remain focused entirely on the student instead of the parents. It is this student-first approach that defines the Student School. The curriculum has been designed to deal with issues that personally affect the students: classes such as gay and lesbian studies, food science, and Native studies are among those offered. The overall atmosphere is one of tolerance, and the students respond to it. In the entire history of the school, not one violent incident has ever been reported. And when John met with the parents of failing students to give them the bad news, the parents often were just grateful that their child had actually stayed in school until November for the first time in years.

John believes teenagers have very strong consciences; while they are not always brimming with optimism, they do want to make a difference. Encouraging kids to act on their social conscience is, to him, one of the best ways the Student School can live up to its "alternative" label. One example is the time the students received permission to put together a political science conference to take a critical look at multinational corporations such as Coca-Cola and Wal-Mart. They chose the theme, created brochures, invited guests, and even brought in students from other schools. As a result of what the kids learned, the Student School became one of the first schools to collectively ban Coke. This co-operation between students and teachers is another key aspect of the school's "alternative" focus: by placing important decisions back into the hands of the students, they are encouraged to participate in the system that will help shape their future.

When John retired, an event was held at the Student School to mark the occasion. A mural depicting various aspects of the Student School's message and mission — a replica of which John keeps in his living room — was unveiled in the front lobby. Former students, some from as far back as fifteen years, returned to the school to pay tribute to him. Some thanked him for saving them, others were grateful he had given them direction. John is strongly affected by the fact that he has made such an impact on his students — but what fills him with the most contentment are the accomplishments that he, his colleagues, his friends, and his students at the Student School built together.

SHAWN "BLU" ROSE

The blue skies of winter will always remind Janette Rose of her son, Shawn. The boy loved blue, she remembers; it was his favourite colour. His friends used to call him "Blu." She was not partial to nicknames, but "Blu" means a lot to her.

⟝⟞

SHAWN D. ROSE was born at sunrise on November 27, 1976, and died at sunset on November 7, 2005. In his twenty-eight years, he had emerged as a promising young leader who encouraged the youth in his community to strive for the best in themselves. Employed by the City of Toronto Parks and Recreation Department, he touched many souls and changed how his friends, family, and the youth he worked with felt about themselves. He instilled hope in those around him and inspired his peers to chase their dreams, because anything was possible if they believed in it.

Shawn's family came to Toronto on March 2, 1975, from Guyana. His grandfather arrived first, to take up a job at a furniture factory. When the rest of the family arrived, they first set up in the Bridle-towne Circle area of Scarborough before moving to Malvern. All three generations of the family lived together in the same house, which Janette believes had a profound influence on her son's up-bringing. Because his grandfather provided affection and took an interest in his life, Shawn internalized a love for youth that led him to become passionately involved in kids' programs at the Malvern Community Centre. His love of reading was instilled at a very young age by his grandmother, who taught him that reading was learning; when she read to him his face would light up with interest and curiosity.

Janette, too, was a strong source of guidance. She told her kids that there are two roads: a straight road and a winding road. If they picked the winding road, they would be on their own — any police officers who called about them would be told to keep them.

One of the most important lessons Shawn learned from his mother was the importance of being a leader and not a follower. She knew he had ideas and could see he was becoming an outspoken young man. But he was a good listener, and wouldn't hesitate to ask for advice. He was also persistent: Janette recalls him coming home and crying when he didn't receive responses for job applications. He did not give up easily nor did he stop trying. It was important to Shawn that his mother be proud of him. He saw her as a hard-working single mom and wanted to give back, promising to never leave her alone.

When Shawn was twelve, Janette took him to Guyana, where he discovered a passion for that country's culture and people. By the end of the trip he had made many new friends, and he called everyone he saw his "cousins." This notion of community as family — and family as community — became Shawn's ideal for civic life when he returned to Toronto. Janette remembers how he would come home from his job at the recreation centre and check in on everyone in the family, interviewing them on how their day went, what they accomplished, and whether they were achieving what they wanted. He would often stay behind at work and do the same with the kids there, talking about life issues and helping them with what they should stay focused on, what mattered in life, and what didn't.

The goals of others were also important to him. Shawn told the kids he worked with that they could be anything they wanted to be. He told his sister the exact same thing — and when she received an entrance scholarship to the University of Nebraska, he reassured his mother that the risks of living alone in another country were secondary to her daughter's dream.

After finishing high school, Shawn went to Centennial College to study business administration. He grew to realize, however, that what he really wanted to do was become a senior youth worker. The local school board had already picked up on his talent for keeping kids on the right track. They turned problem students over to Shawn, because they knew that kids responded well to him.

He lived at home through his mid-twenties, working towards a job with the city. Once he'd secured a career, his plan was to marry Lindsay Jupiter, his high school sweetheart and girlfriend of twelve years, then go back to Centennial and take a special youth program. Unfortunately, this was not meant to be.

On Saturday, November 6, 2005, around nine p.m., Janette noticed that her house was unusually cold. She went downstairs to check on the furnace, called the repairmen, and then joined her cousin in the kitchen for a snack. As they entered the room, she

suddenly heard a loud crash from upstairs. It was Shawn. She found him lying on the floor in front of his grandfather's bedroom. He asked her to call 911, explaining that he had a massive migraine on one side of his head. He tried to get up, but fell back to the floor.

As Janette placed a call to 911, Shawn started sweating and his nose began to bleed. He was unresponsive by the time the ambulance arrived. They took him to Sunnybrook Hospital, where the emergency doctor told her that her son had suffered an aneurysm, resulting from a tangled blood vessel that had been present since birth. Their plan was to go in to see if they could stop the bleeding, but the prognosis would have been poor even if they had discovered the condition early.

The doctor escorted her to the Intensive Care Unit, where one look at Shawn told her just how grave his condition was. He was on life support. A large tube ran down his windpipe and a smaller line ran up through his nose and down into his stomach; his contagious energy and spark of life had been replaced by the rhythmic sounds of a ventilator.

Meanwhile, a friend who heard the news was downstairs making calls, getting the word out that Shawn was fighting for his life at Sunnybrook Hospital. Within half an hour, 150 young people were gathered in the lobby to set up camp. They were not going to let their friend, their captain, go without rallying for him.

A nurse came to the ICU and told Janette about the group in the lobby. She joined them, consoling them even as she cried with them, as the doctors performed the emergency operation. Though she was informed that Shawn had very little chance of making it, Janette held on to her belief in God and hoped for a miracle. She then went home to rest for a few hours. At midnight, the hospital called. Shawn had suffered a massive stroke.

The next day felt odd. The hope and adrenaline that had fuelled her the previous day had burned off. When Janette reached the hospital, the ICU doctor told her they wanted to take Shawn off the ventilator to see how he would do. Unfortunately, the stroke had left extensive brain damage and he would never again enjoy his previous quality of life. The best-case scenario would be chronic care and a life spent in the hospital. As she watched her son struggle off the ventilator, unable to sustain himself, Janette made an impossible choice and decided to allow nature to take its course. A nurse replaced his sedative with a morphine drip, and at sunset, Shawn slipped away.

On Saturday, November 12, the Church of the Nativity on Sewell Road overflowed with mourners, including me. The service was a testament to the relationships that Shawn had fostered with the young people of his community, which was summed up by a poem read at the service. The poem's title was "Blu Rose" and it was about "a rose that had many stems that branched out to the rest."

After the funeral, local councillor Raymond Cho asked a group of Shawn's friends if there was anything he could do. All they asked was that a park be named after him. A public consultation was held in March, where more than two hundred citizens spoke of Shawn in high regard, and a petition with more than 250 names was signed in favour of the honour. The community's wish was granted on August 13, 2006, when Empringham Park was officially renamed the Shawn "Blu" Rose Park. A touching tribute was paid at the ceremony by one young man, who sang beautifully and movingly. Like many present, I felt a tear run down my cheek as his love for Blu came through in his song.

JANETTE ROSE NEVER pictured having to bury her own son, or crying on the bus every day. But if there is one thing to be gained from her tragedy, it is that before Shawn's passing, she had no idea that he was loved by so many, and wasn't aware of the impact he had on the community. The way the people of Malvern rallied around Shawn at his passing — and continued to honour his memory afterwards — says just as much to her about the community support for her family as it does about the leader her son was.

ANDREW COX

A ndrew Cox believes that absolutely anything is possible. He is an Information Technology technician at Toronto law firm Heenan Blaikie. But in his off-hours, he is Jaydahmann, an up-and-coming hip-hop artist who has been showcased on CBC Radio, has had a number one song on Flow 93.5 FM, and was nominated Canadian hip-hop artist of the year in 2008 by Buffalo radio station WBLK.

Things have not always been this promising. To get to this point, Andrew has had to survive childhood poverty, a violent upbringing, and a stint in jail. He experienced more as a teenager than most people will in their entire lives. He can testify that going straight is not easy — but he knows it is worth it. Despite what he has gone through, all the obstacles he has had to face, Andrew Cox has managed to find his own way.

ANDREW GREW UP in the Jane and Finch area in a three-bedroom townhouse complex on Shoreham Drive. Anywhere from twelve to fifteen people occupied the complex at any given time, including his mother, grandmother, siblings, aunt, uncle, and cousin. His father was not there, however; he had separated from Andrew's mother before Andrew was born.

Life was a struggle from as far back as Andrew can remember. He recalls a time when he was six years old and there was not enough food to go around. The family was always short of money, and he was forced to stand aside while his friends joined school clubs, took lessons, and participated in activities. He could not even afford pizza lunches at school.

Andrew's mother was just entering her twenties and already had six children. She was not often around, choosing to go out with friends. With no father at home, Andrew was forced to take responsibility at an early age. He took it upon himself to keep track of where his siblings were in the neighbourhood, and made sure they were ready for school.

Andrew blames his father for not being there when he needed him most; watching his friends get dropped off at school by their dads was a painful reminder of his absence. Instead of the knowledge and wisdom he could have received from his father, Andrew received misguided and faulty advice from friends and older males. The experience taught him that there is no substitute for the wisdom a father can offer a son.

The first defining moment of Andrew's life came when he was six or seven. At that time, his mother was in a relationship with a drug dealer, exposing the children to many dramatic scenes — including more than one occasion when armed men would enter their home to shake down his stepfather.

One particular night, as the family sat around the dinner table,

there was a knock on the door. His mother got up to answer, only to come running back immediately. Masked men with machine guns entered, demanding money, drugs, valuables, and threatening to kill everyone.

The children were ordered into the bathroom. When his little brother would not stop asking what was happening, Andrew knelt with him by the bathtub to pray for the family's safety. When they were finished, they noticed that the door had swung slightly ajar. They peeked through the crack and saw that the gangsters were trashing the home. One of the men spotted the boys and closed the door firmly.

It seemed like forever before their mother finally came for her children. When she did, they could not believe their eyes. She was bleeding. The house was completely wrecked. They did not realize until that moment that they had been held hostage for almost the entire night.

Andrew spent his teen years at St. Leonard's Public School, where he developed an avid interest in basketball. His inspiration was NBA player Allen Iverson. Iverson — like Andrew, the child of a single teenaged mother — often spoke about the deplorable inner-city conditions he'd lived in as a young boy, the abuse he'd experienced, and the absence of his father. Somehow, though, he defied adversity and made it to the pro league.

Andrew's dream was to follow in the footsteps of his hero. He dominated on the local courts, and was the rare shorter player who could slam-dunk on a ten-foot net. His teachers and friends thought he was headed straight to the NBA. Although it was not to be, Andrew wonders now what could have happened if circumstances had been different. Regardless, his passion for basketball served a purpose: it kept him from becoming immersed in deeper trouble. While his friends pursued mischief, he was running to the basketball court. No one ever thought he was a bad kid who should be avoided.

In his last year of high school, Andrew discovered that his favourite subject was law — an interest nurtured by his teacher, Mr. Saker. His basketball coach, Mr. Bruyard, was another big influence. Both men genuinely cared. They recognized his difficult home life, yet never hesitated to push him when he slacked off. They told him he could do and be anything, and helped him believe he had something to offer the world.

When high school was over, Andrew's situation deteriorated. His relationship with his mother, who had begun seeing different men again, was at an all-time low. More significantly, his girlfriend was pregnant. Andrew felt completely lost, caught between the fading hope of an NBA career, the responsibilities of being a young father, and the uncertainty of what to do for a living.

To escape the turmoil at home, Andrew moved back in with his grandparents at Lawrence Heights, but the change of address was not enough to prevent him from getting involved in another kind of trouble. His friends had become involved in illegal activities, and seeing them driving expensive cars had an effect on him. He too began dealing drugs, and eventually found that he was earning enough money to quit his job working for a collection agency.

Things took a turn for the worse when Andrew's brother was charged with homicide. The police began to turn their attention to Andrew, wiretapping the family's phones, suspecting — correctly — that Andrew was storing weapons at his grandparents' house. He was convicted of possession of a sawed-off shotgun and sent to the Maplehurst Correctional Complex for six months, beginning in March 2004.

Survival of the fittest was the rule in prison. The fights were brutal. Fortunately for Andrew, his upbringing on the streets had prepared him to be tough when necessary. He only had to deal with one violent confrontation, and he ended it in such a way that the next day, his attacker sent him an apology along with a chocolate bar and some chips. For the rest of his prison sentence, Andrew was well-behaved. He devoted the time in his cell to intense self-analysis. He analyzed everything: his surroundings, his family, his friends, his relationships, his dreams. He wondered what had happened to his plans to get into university, the night classes he had been taking, all the preparation that had gone to waste.

It was during his time in prison that Andrew began to write lyrics. Putting his thoughts to paper proved to be a therapeutic process. He worked out the confusion of his younger years in his lyrics, referencing issues such as the pain of his childhood and the absence of his father. When he recited his lyrics to the other inmates, they went wild. He had discovered a melody and a beat for life.

Andrew was encouraged. If he could gain people's respect on the inside, he could make it on the outside. He resolved to never go back to jail again. With his music, he hoped to influence inner-city kids, and kids living in social housing. He wanted to show them it was possible to transcend, to have a positive effect, to succeed. He wanted to change the world.

When he was free again, Andrew began working part-time at ING Direct, and sold urban clothing out of his car. He also worked with photographer Rodrigo Moreno on an inspirational youth photography project in Lawrence Heights. Lawrence Heights is a community housing project that is also one of the city's thirteen priority neighbourhoods. A priority neighbourhood is one marked by high levels of poverty and low levels of public investment. The city has made these neighbourhoods a priority for public investment and for innovative programs to provide opportunities for young people. Moreno became a mentor, taking Andrew — whose prior knowledge of the city was restricted to his local neighbourhood — to experience more of Toronto.

One night, Andrew ran into a few friends who were going to a local community centre to check out a program called PAYE — the Partnership to Advance Youth Employment — because it sounded like there was money involved. He remembers tagging along and peeking through a crack in the door. A Trinidadian man spotted him and invited him to join them. Though he was reluctant at first, Andrew eventually went in. What he found was a world of opportunity. Gathered inside were industry leaders, including representatives from the Royal Bank and IBM. Andrew was handed a list of jobs available through the program. He was stunned. He told himself he would not leave until he got his foot in the door somewhere.

Andrew had a brief glimpse at what was possible, but success was not immediate. He went to all the interviews he could, but because of pending charges yet to be cleared up, did not get any calls back. He felt discouraged. Friends from the hood were calling, and the temptation to revert to the way of life he once knew was a strong one. He was considering going back to school when Deborah, a coach from the PAYE program, called. She worked out of St. Stephen's Community House, coaching young candidates like himself to be ready for the workforce, and she wanted him to know that she believed in him. He had left a real impression on his interviewers on the night he attended the program; she thought he was too smart and had too much potential to give up, and was adamant about getting him in somewhere.

The phone call made Andrew reassess his plans. He remembered what it was like growing up with no one to provide for him, and wanted something different for his own two children. Deborah called back with an interview for an internship at the Toronto office of the law firm Heenan Blaikie. The job would not pay well, but Andrew saw it as a way to get in the door.

The interview took place a month later. Andrew's trip downtown turned out to be an eye-opener. It was his first time in a really elegant building, and he was in awe. Andrew had a successful interview, and was offered a position in the information technology department for twelve dollars an hour. The job required hard work and the ability to adapt quickly. Andrew remembers thinking at the time that he would just ride it out and see what would happen. His three-month contract became another three-month contract, and that eventually became a full-time position with a fifty per cent pay increase — and training to become an IT professional.

⊷⊶

ANDREW LOVES HIS job at Heenan Blaikie. Nothing that happens at the firm would be possible without the IT department. Andrew oversees everything from repairing applications and setting up laptops to upgrading software. His department provides a place where he can draw on his strengths and abilities, and his co-workers, aware of the trajectory his life has taken, embrace it with good humour.

The pressures of his old life, however, continue to make themselves felt. As recently as last year, former associates would see him on the street and try to get him to ride with them. It was hard to say no, but Andrew has been saying no for a while, and vows to continue to say no. He wants to show them there are many legitimate ways to make money, and wishes more of them would have faith in the process he went through. Andrew truly believes that people of power can be helpful. He is grateful in particular to Steve Diamond, who championed the PAYE program that turned his life around. And he was thrilled to be invited to the Office of the Mayor and introduced as one of Toronto's success stories at a press conference; he knows that the PAYE program was one of my initiatives.

Andrew is proud of his accomplishments, not just in his career, but as a person. For example, he feels that he treats women much better than he used to, and is proud of the fact that he has become the father his dad never was. Despite what he has gone through, he has managed to find his place — a positive place. He lives in Brampton now, but often goes back to his old community to speak with youth. He knows that his experiences, both good and bad, are ones that his audience can relate to, and he feels he has a lot to teach them. The message he spreads is the same one that changed his life: to look for opportunities and really go after them, even if it means taking a few steps back to go a few steps forward.

NADIA BECKLES

The afternoon of November 18, 2005, when Nadia Beckles found her eighteen-year-old son, Amon, gunned down on the front steps of the West Seventh Day Adventist Church, is one that will remain with her. The chaos of that day has left her with nightmares and a fear of crowds. All she asks for is to be healed; she thinks she's getting there, but the process is slow. Sometimes she wishes she could run away to a place where no one would know where she is and she wouldn't have to hear about crime rates or news of more shootings.

Yet, despite her loss, Nadia has somehow discovered the resolve to be there for others. She is a member of a group called UMOVE (United Mothers Opposing Violence Everywhere, founded by Torontonian Audette Sheppard, whose only son, Justin, was also shot and killed) and helps to provide emotional support to women who have undergone experiences similar to hers. It takes a remarkable person to attend funerals — ones reminding her so poignantly of her own loss — in order to console and reassure women she has never met. Nadia does this willingly.

———◆———

NADIA WAS BORN in Birmingham, England, in 1970. Her father, originally from Barbados, was a soldier in the British army who spoke the Queen's English perfectly and presented as a proper gentleman. Her mother came from Trinidad and Tobago, and had more of a laid-back personality, encouraging son and daughter to experience life more spontaneously.

The family moved to Toronto when Nadia was six years old. Her early years were somewhat sheltered. Nadia always seemed caught between her father's rules and her mother's more carefree and spontaneous approach. It wasn't until she was fifteen and went on a school trip to Trinidad that she experienced any real independence from her family. She fell in love with a boy while she was there, and found herself pregnant upon her return. Fortunately, her parents were nothing but supportive.

As a teenage mother, she needed all the help she could get. Nadia needed to work to take care of her baby, Amon, and was forced to study around her job schedule rather than focus on school as a foundation for a career. She sometimes tried to live on her own in order to feel less like a teenager and more like an independent mother, but she always ended up going back home to her parents.

There were other sources of support aside from the family. When she was still in school, Nadia participated in a program for teenage mothers at Jessie's Centre for Teenagers. She took Amon with her, and recalls participating in cooking classes and other activities;

thanks to the centre, she never felt alone in raising her son.

Eventually, however, Nadia became involved in an abusive relationship. It wasn't until five years had passed and two children were born that she decided to break it off. While it was a difficult time for her family, Nadia believes walking away from that relationship made her stronger and more certain about what she wanted. Rather than just accepting life as it happened, by making her own choice, she was finally ready to participate on an adult level.

Nadia wanted her children to be raised in the same environment of respect as she was. Her father was a big influence in that regard. He often scolded his grandson about his comportment: baggy jeans, for instance, were not allowed in the house, and her father kept a pocketful of twine in order to keep Amon's pants properly on his waist. For Nadia's part, she tried to educate her son about Black culture. She showed him the miniseries *Roots* to inspire him; she also showed him gangster movies to make him aware of what making the wrong choices could lead to. Afterwards, they would sit down and discuss the issues. It was a joy for her to realize that, as the years went by, she was beginning to feel that he taught her just as much as she taught him.

Watching Amon grow was mostly a pleasure. He enjoyed running track and playing baseball, and loved to dance from an early age. Though he was a quiet boy who needed a bit of a push with his studies, Amon was popular with the girls and had no problems making friends in middle school. His best friend and constant companion was a child named Jamal Hemmings. Nadia was friends with Jamal's mother, which helped her to keep track of where her son was. As Amon grew into his late teens, however, watching him became more difficult. He would often be away from the house for most of the day and late into the night.

One afternoon, Nadia's father called with serious news: Jamal had been shot and killed after school near Eglinton Avenue and Oakwood Avenue. Amon had witnessed the murder, and was now with Nadia's parents, who had rushed to collect him from the authorities as soon as the school had called to notify them of the tragedy. Nadia came to pick him up, and Amon ran into her arms; it was the first time she recalled seeing pain in his eyes, and she held him close as they drove home. Neither would be able to sleep that night.

Being a witness put Amon in danger. Because of the lingering threat to his life, the family decided that Amon should keep a low profile. For Jamal's funeral a week after his murder, they thought it best that he stay home while they went in his place. It was an eerie experience. From the minute she entered West Seventh Day Adventist Church, Nadia was extremely uncomfortable. A strange feeling came over her as she studied the faces of the students and friends who had gathered.

At about 12:30, just moments after the minister began the service, the sound of gunfire rang from outside the front doors. The entire congregation from one side of the church rose and raced toward her, like a human tsunami. She became concerned for her children and cousins, and focused on getting them to the floor. Suddenly, a woman screamed Amon's name above the confusion of the crowd. Confused, Nadia moved past the others and made her way outside. Amon lay on the sidewalk, his eyes half open. His grandmother was administering CPR, and told Nadia to apply pressure to the bullet holes. When the paramedics came and placed her son in the back of the ambulance, Nadia remembers noting how little blood there was. Amon never made it to the hospital.

Nadia respects the reason her son went to the funeral: he wanted to prove his worth as a friend, as a man. The honourable thing to do was pay his respects to Jamal instead of cowering in fear. But Amon's death was still devastating. He was not just her son —

he was her best friend, a gentle soul who took good care of her. Fortunately, Nadia discovered she did not have to deal with her loss alone. In the weeks following Amon's funeral, Audette Sheppard and the women of UMOVE contacted her and quickly became a strong force of empathy in her life. She remembers the other mothers were always present, watching over her, and ready to offer support if she needed it. Unlike some other people in her life, the UMOVE people knew that healing would take a long time.

=⊲=

NADIA WILL NEVER forget, and she may never forgive. She wonders when her sorrow will diminish. For now, however, she intends to use her experience to help others. She has become an outspoken advocate against gun violence. Her focus is on creating a safer environment for young people by improving their education. She believes that, in certain ways, the school system has failed children. There should be a return to a more balanced curriculum to give the children more breadth of experience, with less emphasis on sports and more money put into arts, theatre, home economics, and vocational courses like car repair. Also, instead of simply suspending troubled students, schools — and adults in general — need to take a more active role in guiding children. Children can't teach themselves, nor should they teach each other. Nadia knows her son benefited tremendously from the guidance his grandparents gave him.

It is her work with UMOVE, however, that is the most personal, and at the same time, the most selfless. Nadia is a UMOVE mom herself now. She attends funerals even though they remind her of her own son's. She won't tell other mothers what happened to her

— not initially anyway. Instead she holds them, consoles them, even whispers in their ears that she genuinely understands what they are going through. "This is not the time or place to explain myself but one day, I will." She does not know where her strength comes from, but she is always ready to share it.

LIZZ BRIGGS

"Toronto" is an Aboriginal word with several meanings, one of which — "meeting place" — makes the name a fitting one for our city. Even today, it probably has the largest urban aboriginal population of any city in Canada. But what truly makes Toronto an aboriginal city is its history.

Toronto started as the foot of the Carrying Place trail, where the mouth of the Humber lies today. The Carrying Place trail was once used by the First Nations people to trade the abundant goods of the region. Only later did the first European settlers in Canada, the Rousseau family, decide to build their home there.

Yet Toronto does not know itself as an aboriginal city. Certainly, Torontonians know and are proud of the many success stories of Native people who serve as Court of Appeal judges, bankers, artists, singers, and business leaders. They also respect the fact that Native elders often open public events in this city. The most common view of aboriginal people, however, is one of poverty, homelessness, and dislocation — particularly amongst their youth. The incredible strength and resilience of some aboriginal people — even the ones living right in their neighbourhood — is not something most Torontonians are aware of. I am lucky. As mayor of Toronto, I do get to see, and be inspired by, these stories.

—◆—

I MET LIZZ Briggs at an event in Scarborough to organize a Jane's Walk. These walks are named after the great urbanist Jane Jacobs, and are designed to ensure that people get to know each other and their neighbourhod. At the event, Lizz told me how a debate arose at an earlier meeting about what colour the buttons for the Scarborough area should be, and how she made a strong, impassioned case that the colour should be blue. It was then that I first saw the quiet depth and philosophical background that Lizz, like many Native people in our city, possesses. This depth extends to her life story. While it does feature hardship and perseverance, it is — more than anything — a story that embodies the universal quest for "home."

Lizz was privately adopted into a Caucasian family when she was ten months old. Most of what she remembers as a child is from life in Mississauga. Though at times the environment was very cold, Lizz thinks her adoptive parents are good people and she's sure they tried the best they could, in their own way. She was always provided for and taught the proper things, like how important getting an education was and how to behave at the dinner table.

One poignant memory she has is from when she was about eight years old. While pushing her younger brother in his stroller, she leaned down and whispered to him "I will take care of you — nothing will happen to you."

It was also at this time that she was given a copy of Maurice Sendak's classic children's book, *Where the Wild Things Are*, which was about how a lonely, angry child was able to deal with his demons by turning to the power of imagination. The story played a curious subtext for Lizz's own search for home. At nighttime, Lizz would dream that she too could go on a magical voyage and change the outcome of her life.

Another of Lizz's most valuable possessions was a beaded hair brooch, left for her by her birth mother and given to her by her adoptive mother. The beads on the charm were green, purple, and pink, which she later learned were the colours of her reserve. The brooch also came with a book that was written in Ojibway and English.

Lizz was caught between two versions of what "home" could mean. She had heard that she was originally from White Fish Lake First Nation, just west of Sudbury, but she had no concept of the place, aside from her adopted parents saying that things weren't good where she had come from, and that they wanted a better life for her and didn't want her to end up like her real mom. Her parents also told her that she might embarrass her brothers if she attended the same school as them, because the other kids would find out she was not their real sister.

The more she was confronted with the truth about who she was, the more she had to find a release for her growing anger. At fourteen, she ran away. She was sent to a group home, was and eventually placed in a group home near Runnymede and Bloor.

Lizz spent the next few years in and out of school, spending much of her time on the Parkdale bar scene. She shot pool for money

and drinks, and got good at it, but decided to quit one day when she walked into a room above the pool parlour and discovered a dead body.

At eighteen, she found herself pregnant and — unable to comprehend the responsibilities motherhood required — felt helpless.

It was about this time that Lizz began researching her roots. She travelled to Ottawa to get her Indian Status, and to find out where her home community was. It would be a while before she learned the results of the investigation; in the meantime, she decided to try and find out what being "Indian" meant by visiting the Anishnawbe Health Centre on Toronto's Queen Street. As she walked in her surroundings went into slow motion. She was instantly transfixed by the scent of the smoke inside. The room started to spin and, with her heart beating in her ears, she ran out. The scent was from burning sage and the smell of the medicine had triggered what she describes as a blood memory — an acute experience of who she was, all at once. It felt like home.

After learning how the clan system worked, Lizz was finally able to find information about her mother from the Indian Affairs office. She read through various articles and discovered that her birth name was Nichnawbe Quay, which meant "Aboriginal woman"; that she was from Atikmishing, or "White Fish Lake"; and that her clan was the Loon Clan. She reached out to the stories and lessons offered to her by the community. Her elders also bestowed upon her a spirit name, Biimgut Miptood Myiingan, or "the name speaks of many things that run with wolves." They encouraged her to reach further into the spirit world for direction; she says it was like a bunch of spirits calling her home. But "home" also meant she would eventually have to make the journey back to Sudbury to meet her birth mother.

In November of 2006, Lizz set out on a journey to see her mother for the first time since she was ten months old. A great aunt had told

her, cryptically, that she would find her mother in downtown Sudbury at the Algoma Hospital. Worried her mother might be dying,
Lizz rushed to the facility, where hospital information directed her to
the psychiatric ward. She found her mother sitting in a chair in a
tiny, nondescript room. Despite having been absent for most of
Lizz's life, her mother had an inkling of who she was. Gently, Lizz
told her story, after which her mother rose from the chair and wrapped
her arms around her. At that moment, Lizz Briggs became Lizz
Nootchtai once again, and all the tears of a lost and lonely childhood
became tears of recognition and forgiveness. She offered to take her
mother outside; and as they walked down the dreary hospital halls
and out into the light, Lizz explained how, for as long as she could
remember, she'd preferred being outdoors, standing on the earth.

Meeting her mother allowed Lizz to begin to heal. It also inspired
her to put into practice her passion for sharing what "home" now
means to her, by reaching out to other Native families in Toronto.
When I met her in the spring of 2008, Lizz was working at Native
Child and Family Services, an organization that helps young
aboriginal Canadians discover their identities and heal trauma they
may have suffered in their lives.

Thanks to her quest to discover her roots, Lizz Briggs knows who
she is and where she came from. But it is not how she identifies
herself that makes her an example of the resilience of our aboriginal
people — rather, it is the work she does with Native Child and Family
Services, the work she does every day in the community, and the
work she does every day as the happily married mother of a large
family, that truly demonstrates the ongoing relevance and signifi-
cance of First Nations values and traditions.

TANTAWY ATTIA

September 11, 2001, changed the way the Islamic community is perceived around the world. As a result of the terrorist attacks, Muslim organizations, especially in the United States, have been cast in a negative light. But the support that Toronto provides for its growing Muslim community has never wavered. There is no better example of this than the fact that mere months after 9/11, Dr. Tantawy Attia and his organization, Masjid Toronto, were able to celebrate the founding of a mosque at Dundas and Chestnut, right behind Toronto's City Hall.

⋙

LIFE IN TORONTO had been good from the moment Tantawy arrived. After completing a degree in nuclear engineering at Alexandria University in his home country of Egypt, he received a scholarship

from McMaster for his Ph.D. and moved to Hamilton. In 1976, his academic supervisor found him an opening at Ontario Hydro, and immediately after being hired Dr. Attia relocated to Toronto.

Dr. Attia saw Toronto as a tolerant place where he could practise his faith and pass it on to his nine children. He never encountered any major problems establishing himself as a Muslim, and many aspects of the Canadian welfare system reminded him of how things are expected to run in an Islamic state, where Muslim rulers are expected to feed the poor, provide them with shelter, and look after their health — all goals that Ontario's housing associations, Toronto's social service programs, and Canada's universal health care strive for.

Another aspect of Toronto that appealed to Dr. Attia was its burgeoning Muslim community. As early as 1911, the first Islamic organization, the Muslim Society of Toronto, was established by a group of Albanian Muslims, and in the 1960s, the community as a whole began to flourish when Jami Mosque was set up at Bloor and Dundas. Toronto now has over a hundred mosques of different sizes.

When Dr. Attia moved to Toronto, he joined the Jami Mosque. It did not take long for him to wind up on their board of directors, exposing him to the politics involved in running a mosque for the first time. A troubling parking issue had come up: on the Friday days of prayer, chaos would ensue as cars lined up on both sides of the road and spilled into neighbouring areas. Just a few months in, he began receiving complaints from some of the neighbours, who put together a petition to address the issue. It was hard not to believe that there was an undertone of discrimination in the complaints, which had only arisen after a wave of Somali refugees joined the mosque — changing the race of the worshippers from mostly Caucasian to mostly Black.

Police Superintendent Keith Forde and I spoke to the community. We made the case that what takes place outside the mosque on Friday afternoons is exactly the same as what takes place outside a church on Sunday mornings, or outside any religious institution on their designated day of worship; all the mosque was asking for was equal treatment. When the opponents in the community came forward one last time, concerned that the Friday parking situation constituted a fire hazard, the mosque staged a fire drill that proved fire engines could get through without any problems. After that, things calmed down.

Another of the glaring issues Dr. Attia encountered as the Muslim community continued to grow in the 1990s was that Muslim professionals who worked downtown did not have a place to pray. The solution at the time was to meet in a space at the University of Toronto for Friday prayers. Unfortunately, as the community grew the space became more cramped, and the university began asking people for student identification before allowing them access. Dr. Attia searched for places they could use on Friday afternoons, but the cost of renting for even a few hours was too prohibitive for that solution to be workable. Eventually, he and his colleagues at the Muslim Association of Canada discussed the idea of establishing a permanent mosque in downtown Toronto.

Based on the history of the Jami Mosque, Dr. Attia knew that opening a mosque downtown was going to be difficult. It had taken the financial and political support of the king of Saudi Arabia to help get Jami set up. Still, there was no way he could have foreseen what would eventually become his biggest obstacle. For their site, the Masjid group had selected an old Royal Bank building near City Hall. They were within days of completing the paperwork when the unthinkable happened: the World Trade Center was attacked.

Just hours later, he received a message that the property had received a "more attractive" offer.

It appeared certain that he and his volunteer committee might have to begin a new search. Fortunately, however, the bank called again a few months later. It said that the other bidder's financing had collapsed, and the building was back on the market. Dr. Attia moved swiftly to close the deal, and by January 2002 Masjid Mosque was on the location.

I have been to the mosque often. It is more than a place of worship; it is also a place of lively discussion, debate, and education. For example, during the 2006 city election, I was speaking with a group of worshippers outside the mosque after Friday prayers. One of the worshippers started to condemn same sex marriage as against the Holy Book. Another interrupted him and said, "We may not agree, but we must support their rights. If we do not support their rights, how can we expect people to support ours?"

In addition to serving as the executive director of Masjid Toronto, Dr. Attia sits as a public member on the council of the College of Physicians and Surgeons of Ontario. Because of his science career, he is frequently offered promotions that require a move away from Toronto. He does not consider these offers — nor does he ever think about returning to the Middle East. Going back would land him more money, but at the expense of the freedoms he enjoys here. Toronto means too much to him. It has allowed him to realize his dream of raising his children as Muslims in safety, and guaranteed them the chance for a higher education and professional degrees. Most of all, it is a place that respects and values the rights of all; that in itself makes living in this city priceless.

MOHAMED GILAO

When the phone rang at three a.m. on August 8, 2005, Mohamed Gilao was still half-dreaming. By the time the Toronto police officer on the line had apologized in advance for what he was about to say, however, he was wide awake. The officer told Mohamed that his son, Loyan, had been shot in the chest outside the Phoenix nightclub. His son's friend, Ali Mohamud Ali, had been shot in the head. Both young men were dead.

Mohamed experienced a blinding flash that changed his world forever. This tragedy was not supposed to take place here: Toronto was supposed to be a refuge, the place where his family had escaped the atrocities taking place in Somalia.

MOHAMED GILAO WAS born in Mogadishu, Somalia. He says his memories of the place exist like the flicker of a Super 8 film, rich in colour and dreamlike. He had seven siblings: four brothers and three sisters. His father worked for the United States Aid's procurement department; his mother was a nurse. His grandfather was one of the pioneers of Somali independence and, as a member of parliament in 1956, helped steer the country through post-colonial strife while it broke away from its status as an Italian and British protectorate.

Mohamed was closest to his mother, who was the centre of his family, a role common to most mothers in Somalia. She taught him the importance of duty and family with one simple lesson: family is community and community is family.

It was not until the mid-eighties that Mohamed would draw upon the full depth of his mother's message. At the time he was studying in Rome, a place he now sees as a natural extension of the Catholic influences he experienced in southern Somalia. He focused on the study of sedimentation, with hopes of completing a doctorate in geology. But that all changed when his homeland was plunged into civil war.

From the late eighties onwards, his grandfather's dream of a free and democratic Somali state crumbled. Mohamed witnessed wave after wave of his people being displaced, hundreds of thousands caught in refugee camps while losing their families, their homes, and almost everything they had.

His mother summoned him with an assignment far more urgent and challenging than any Ph.D. She tasked him with rescuing their family from the certain storm in Mogadishu, and ensuring that they were all reunited in Canada. Mohamed abandoned his research and his dream of a career at the University of Mogadishu's Department of Sedimentology, and began to mastermind the escape from Somalia. It was a monumental task. While studying in Rome, Mohamed had worked part-time for Amnesty International and had learned that Canada did not have an embassy in Somalia, and that the best way into our country would be through the United States.

Toronto was the city of choice for Mohamed's mother and family in Canada. One of Mohamed's brothers had already landed an engineering contract here. There also was a burgeoning Somali community that made the city sensitive to what was happening back home. Mohamed was excited about the opportunities that Canada offered his family. Places like Italy, for example, offered very little in comparison. Few countries had the capacity to welcome refugees because of their limited resources or their foreign policies. Canada, however, was multicultural, and Toronto in particular was known for having good programs for immigrants wishing to settle, making communities like his own possible. He wanted to integrate easily, while still maintaining aspects of his own culture, religion, traditions, values, and sense of community. No other country offered these possibilities.

In 1990, Mohamed made his first trip to Canada, accompanied by eight-year-old Loyan. They arrived in Toronto and saw exactly what his mother had envisioned for them: a safe place of opportunity. He knew he needed to bring the rest of his family to the city as soon as possible, because Somalia had collapsed into civil war. Mohamed returned to Mogadishu at the very height of the bloodshed; the scene was disturbing — all of his family's assets were gone, nothing was left.

It took three long years, but by 1994 Mohamed had arranged for his entire family to leave the ruins of Mogadishu and come to the peaceful shores of Lake Ontario. Their lives would begin again.

Shortly after he arrived in Toronto, some local Somalis called

Mohamed. They had caught wind of his story and wanted to see if he would join a community project that was helping newcomers out of East Africa. He did more than help; he turned the project into a full-fledged organization. Inspired by his grandfather's political strength, he worked hard and eventually became the executive director of *Dejinta Beesha*, one of the most established Somali community organizations of its kind in North America.

Mohamed was thrilled that official Toronto was asking for him to share his knowledge to help foster the Somali community. We had a chance to meet when I was the Metro councillor for High Park. Mohamed later told me he was impressed by my commitment to community and family, and, more poignantly, that we had something in common: we were both adult men, fulfilling dreams we shared with our mothers. We eventually worked together on community programs, including our first project, "Somali Week." Apparently my love of sports inspired Mohamed to start his own football program for Somali youth. Mohamed became the resource in Canada for all issues related to the Somali community. His life in Toronto was going splendidly.

In the summer of 2005, Mohamed received devastating news from Mogadishu. His good friend, Abdulkadir Yaha, had been murdered by Islamic extremists. Twelve men had broken into his bedroom in the middle of the night and shot him repeatedly as he lay next to his wife. He had been the director of the Centre for Research and Dialogue in Somalia, a peace leader who was seen to have Western links.

Mohamed reached out to friends and family to help them cope with the assassination. On Sunday, August 7, he hosted a big farewell dinner party for some guests. His son did not attend; Loyan had helped organize a wedding that had just gone off without a hitch, and was with his cousin for one last night out.

In retrospect, Loyan's absence from the dinner party was just one of a number of odd circumstances Mohamed noticed in the week leading up to his son's death. He remembers feeling oddly out of touch with Loyan over those few days. They had, for instance, somehow missed their regular Wednesday coffee. These coffee meetings were not fancy affairs; they usually went to a donut shop near York University's Glendon Campus to talk father-and-son matters. During a coffee meeting several weeks earlier, Mohamed learned that his son dreamed of becoming a detective, like his maternal grandfather had been before becoming a general; he recalls telling Loyan that his dream could well come true because in Canada he had the opportunity to become whatever he wanted. On a later occasion, Loyan cried in gratitude as he realized how fortunate he was to have a father of such strong character who fed his own interest in community and family. Mohamed knew that he was his son's hero; he now wishes he had the chance to tell him his son was his hero.

The missed Wednesday meeting was unusual. Mohamed understood that his son was completely focused on planning the wedding, as he took his best man duties very seriously. But their Wednesday coffee meeting was a ritual they had practised ever since they arrived in Toronto. Looking back, he finds it odd that Loyan had missed it on that particular week.

He remembers, too, that the summer of 2005 was particularly dangerous; it seemed young people were being shot every day. On the night of the dinner party, an uncle had warned Loyan not to go out. Two nights later, he became another statistic of that summer.

Mohamed wonders how things would have turned out if he had had coffee with his son that week. Perhaps that would have steered things differently. Simple yet profound questions occupied him when it felt like everything he had worked for — the dream of Toronto,

his mother's vision — had all collapsed in an instant.

Daily news can still be traumatic for Mohamed. Every new gun tragedy triggers an emotional storm for him. He has become a staunch supporter of anti-gun laws and follows the statistics closely. Each shooting forces him to revisit his own loss and ask both old and new questions about his son's still-unsolved case. Spiritually, the death of his son has demanded more from Mohamed than any other challenge in his life.

Despite experiencing his darkest days in Toronto, Mohamed has never stopped seeing it as a place of hope. He does not regret his decision to come here. While the situation in Somalia remains much as it was in 1989, Toronto has allowed him spiritual growth. He now feels, without a doubt, that he believes in God. The Muslim community has given him much of the strength to carry on. Most of his healing has come from the fact that the values he first learned in Somalia, of community as family, exist in Toronto as well. When his daughter graduated from the University of Toronto in 2009, he was able to celebrate her achievement even in the face of loss.

The day after Loyan died, a visitor appeared at the Gilaos' front door at five in the afternoon. Mohamed felt his son's absence as he made his way past grieving relatives and neighbours towards the front door. Overcome with emotion, his eyes met with the visitor's. I had come to grieve with my friend and was standing in the doorway of his home.

I was with him again after the 2005 Boxing Day murder of Jane Creba, a tragedy that left Mohamed devastated and reduced to tears. Jane, like Loyan, was a promising young person, a leader respected by friends and community. Mohamed felt the same for the Creba family's loss as he had for his own. He stood next to me at the candlelight memorial. During my speech, I lit a candle for Loyan as well. Mohamed later told me that was the moment he truly felt I was grieving not just as a concerned politician, but as a father, and that this kind of caring was part of the fabric of Canada.

Mohamed experienced a long period of darkness after his son's funeral. What helped break the melancholy was a memory of the evening his son invited him to be the guest speaker at York University to address the Somali student association and share his story. It was after this occasion that Loyan expressed how lucky he was to have Mohamed as a resource, and as his father. Remembering that moment was an awakening; it reconnected Mohamed to a purpose he had forgotten in his grief: his community in Toronto still needed his leadership. Despite losing Loyan — whose name means "loyalty" — Mohamed's hope and commitment to his mission have grown even stronger.

TRISH MAHTANI

The Gerrard India Bazaar is a small group of businesses on Gerrard Street, stretching between Coxwell Avenue and Greenwood Avenue. The bazaar is famous internationally for its unique blend of shops and restaurants. With businesses of Bangladeshi, Pakistani, Gujarati, Punjabi, Hindu, Sikh, and Muslim backgrounds, this strip of Gerrard is practically a microcosm of the Indian subcontinent. The businesses have worked together to create a Business Improvement Area, or BIA. A BIA is a partnership between businesses — who collectively agree to a levy (a voluntary tax) — and the City of Toronto, which matches the investment of the businesses. These investments could be physical improvements — like benches or flowers — or promotional activities — like hosting festivals. The BIA concept started in Toronto (in Bloor West Village) and has now spread around the world.

Two shops in particular serve as an example of the entrepreneurial spirit that drives the bazaar. Nucreation, an Indian clothing store owned by Govind Mahtani, is an explosion of colour on the north side of Gerrard. It specializes in wedding clothes, and customers from all over North America shop to buy innovative design and affordable quality. Right across the street is Rang, an interior décor shop owned by Mahtani's daughter, Trish, who makes Canadian-style bedding from Indian fabrics. Their story is not one of rags-to-riches; rather, it is about how a family — and a community — can grow together in Toronto.

GOVIND MAHTANI LEARNED business from his father and helped him run a modest retail operation in Mumbai, but it was not until he was living in Hong Kong with his Japanese wife and their five children that he experienced his own success. They did very well, helped by a healthy mail-order business and reasonable rents. As the children approached university age, however, the family had a dilemma: Hong Kong at the time had only one university. If all five children were to go to school, they would have to go overseas, which was an option the family could not afford without relocating. Mahtani decided a move to Canada would be the best solution; his children could pursue their desired educations, and he could develop his business. He considered Quebec and Vancouver, but because one of the boys was interested in an engineering program at the University of Toronto, our city became the final choice.

The family arrived in 1982. Mahtani started his retail trade by selling saris imported from his Japan and Hong Kong network. He

began bringing in items from India — expanding that part of the business in 1989 — and by the next year had established a full retail operation on Gerrard Street, selling Indian formal wear.

Trish, who was only nine years old when the family left Hong Kong, spent most of her adolescent years adjusting to her new surroundings. Life in Toronto's Leslie and Lawrence area was much different from what she'd known. The family picnics she'd enjoyed in Japan were a thing of the past, as were the adventures she'd had in Hong Kong's Kowloon area. Her new peers mostly wanted to go to malls and hang out — an activity her parents considered pointless. Trish herself was divided; there were aspects of the more independent Canadian childhood that were liberating, and aspects that seemed disrespectful.

Having spent so much time around her father, Trish found herself naturally leaning towards business and economics by the time she finished high school. She craved more independence, and so went to the University of Western Ontario for Administrative and Commercial Studies. After graduation, Trish was not sure what she wanted to do for a living. Accounting was an option, but it did not prove nearly as interesting to her as she had hoped. She had a talk with her parents about possibly getting involved with Nucreation. Her father said she could try it out.

Trish started out at the family business dealing hands-on with customers, and eventually became involved with purchasing as well. When her father needed to take a business trip to India, he encouraged her to accompany him to get a better grasp of what she was getting involved in. The three weeks they spent travelling, from Delhi to Jaipur to her father's hometown of Mumbai, were an eye-opening experience.

A particularly memorable moment took place in a New Delhi market when Trish wandered into a small room in a back area and discovered six people embroidering the most beautiful fabric she had ever seen. It was a type of handcrafting, involving unique textiles and fabrics, that she had never seen in Canada. She found the amount of work that went into each product, and the fact that they were being created from scratch, inspiring; this — coupled with the responsibility that her father had given her to make independent decisions about fabric — helped make up her mind about what she was going to do.

When they got back to Toronto, Trish told her family that she wanted to run her own home décor business. They were, as always, supportive. She began by selling custom bedsheets at her father's store, and by 2005 was able to open her own shop across the street.

Despite being divided between two businesses, the Mahtani family ties remain strong. Trish's mother brings her coffee every morning, and the entire family tries to get together on Sundays, even if it just means hanging out in either of the stores. Theirs is a camaraderie that extends over the rest of the Gerrard India Bazaar. For example, one of the goals of the bazaar is to get more people in Toronto interested in the small business collectively, so in the third week of August, all of the stores participate in an event that attracts increasing numbers of people every year. What comes naturally for the Mahtanis is now something that all of the diverse shopkeepers of the Gerrard India Bazaar embrace: everyone working in the best interests of one another, even if they are in competition.

RITA COX

Storytelling is in Rita Cox's blood. It was a vital part of her upbringing in Trinidad, where her mother often used proverbs and adages both to teach and to scold. Rita knows that storytelling is the most powerful way to impart transformative lessons; it is a huge reason why she chose to become a children's librarian. Just as tales of Anansi, a Caribbean folk hero, helped Rita's people overcome oppression, so too can her own tale — that of a woman who left her homeland and, by doing what she loves, became instrumental in revitalizing an entire community — help newcomers become aware of the possibilities life in Toronto has to offer.

RITA'S FATHER WAS a school principal, her mother a teacher. They were a big reason why she had such an insatiable imagination — from the very beginning of her life, Rita's parents read to her and told her stories. Her eldest brother, too, was a huge influence. It was from him that she received her first book, *The Story of Grace Darling.*

As a child she was a self-described "reading fool," often so engrossed with a book that she would hide under the dining room table and not come out until she had finished it. At the age of ten she could most often be found hanging around the local library. Having read through the entire children's collection, she was eventually allowed access to the adult section — she saw it as a rite of passage, an early graduation.

Hers was a story-based culture, and the other children were also immersed in stories. They would often play games revolving around Anansi, a West African spider god who was brought to the New World by slaves and transformed into a trickster figure. In the stories, Anansi was a small, weak character who always managed to outwit larger, more powerful creatures. Looking back, Rita marvels at how important these tales were in helping her ancestors come together to survive oppression.

One of the most important times of Rita's life took place when her hometown library opened a new children's section and invited a special visitor named Augusta Baker to fly down to Trinidad. Baker was the children's literature coordinator at a large public library in Manhattan and had arranged to stay in Rita's town for a couple of months to help reorganize their library.

Baker ran story hours every Saturday back in New York, and decided to do the same in Trinidad. Rita would sit mesmerized as Baker read to her and the other children, and an interest grew in her that went beyond the stories. When volunteers were asked to come to the library and tell stories, the adults were reluctant, but Rita and other youngsters jumped at the opportunity to be just as spellbinding as Baker. Schools were invited to come in and watch as the young "pages" told stories. After one of the sessions, Baker told Rita that she had a gift for storytelling that she needed to own. It was then that Rita knew she wanted to be a children's librarian.

When Baker left Trinidad, Rita decided to follow in her footsteps. She worked in the library all through high school. After graduating she began looking into attending school in England, but Augusta Baker — who kept in touch with the Coxes — invited her to New York instead. It was a dream come true. Rita went to Columbia University, where Baker was teaching, and learned that her mentor was famous, regarded as the "lioness" of children's literature in America.

Rita's earliest days in New York remain a vivid memory. Never in her life had she seen as many lights as she did the night her plane landed in the city. Her aunt and uncle greeted her at the airport; she stayed with them, attending classes and working part-time at the main library at 42nd Street and Fifth Avenue. Those first few months were a time of wonder. Rita recalls the day her aunt called her at work and told her to look outside, causing her to run out into the library's back garden to experience snow for the first time.

Tragedy struck in 1959 when, just a year into Rita's studies, her mother fell ill. Rita returned to Trinidad, but her mother passed away within a year. It was a difficult period. Instead of returning to New York, Rita applied for an opening at the Toronto Public Library. Her studies had already taken her to Toronto to study the Osborne Collection of Children's Literature, and she had fallen in love with the city and its public library system. She jumped at the chance and got the position. Upon arrival back in Toronto, she found a small contingent of representatives from the library waiting for her at the airport. They whisked her down to Yonge and College for lunch before taking her to her residence at the YWCA on Woodlawn Avenue.

It was not until she entered her room that Rita realized she was on her own for the first time in her life. When she was in New York, she'd had her aunt and uncle — as well as Augusta Baker — to watch out for her. The thought of being alone was overwhelming. But when she saw a huge arrangement of flowers on her table, with a tag that read "Welcome to the Toronto Public Library," she felt reassured that she had arrived in a wonderful situation after all.

In addition to her job as children's librarian at the Charles G. Fraser School, Rita found work at the Boys and Girls House on St. George Street. She spent the rest of her time at the University of Toronto in order to continue her graduate studies with its renowned Osborne Collection of Early Children's Literature. Afterwards, she pursued a Ph.D. in New York, but always returned home to Toronto.

She was eventually transferred to the Gerrard branch of the Toronto Public Library. She became familiar with the children of the local schools and would lead them in many activities, including drama and puppetry. Rita loved her job, and grew close to the teachers and other librarians. In less than a year, however, she was asked to take over leadership of the Parkdale Branch. She did not want to go, but Alice Kane, her mentor in Toronto, convinced her that Parkdale needed her talents. So, in August 1972, Rita took the position. It was a decision that would, eventually, help her realize her full potential, and one she would hold for a very long time — including through the election of a young Metro councillor for Parkdale.

By the time I was first elected in 1994, Rita was a legend as the librarian for the Parkdale Library at Queen and Cowan, and was nearing the end of her career. The library was the hub of activity in

the community. Meetings of every kind — including political — were held there every night, and the library, part of the best and busiest library system in the world, was a place of welcome to literally everyone: homeless people, survivors of the mental health system, newcomers ... The wonderfully diverse families that make up Parkdale are fierce advocates for various important causes — and children.

Parkdale was, from the beginning, a challenging place to work. Since Rita's job was to serve the needs of the community, she did her best to learn everything she could about its politics. She also got involved in every organization she could, from the taxpayers' association, to the schools, to the legal aid groups. In doing so, Rita occasionally found herself up against what she called the "western guard" of eastern European men who were not used to taking orders from a Black woman. At one meeting, she was even accused of being a communist because of her work with the community centre.

Fortunately, her work took place at a time when volunteerism and social activism were at an all-time high. Canada's centennial celebration had created an atmosphere of optimism and action that continued through the seventies. One of the gifts to Toronto in 1967 was from the Caribbean community, based on the Trinidadian tradition of carnival: Caribana. Such signs of Toronto's growing diversity helped Rita begin to make headway in the community. With the support of many community members, she spearheaded the drive to form an intercultural council for Parkdale.

But it was at the library that she did her most notable work. She pioneered a number of marvellous programs that got children to actively participate in books and reading. As the Librarian in Parkdale, Rita would read children stories with a wonderful voice and a loving spirit. One summer, her Ogopogo Club — a club named after the legendary Canadian lake monster, that Rita used to bring together children from different cultural backgrounds — built an arts and crafts model of their namesake that was so large it stretched along the top shelves throughout the library. Another summer she ran a program called "In Gramma's Country," which asked children to share stories, recipes, and other wisdom taught to them by their grandmothers.

Before Rita came along, none of the libraries in the Toronto system had literacy programs or information centres. She succeeded in transforming her library from a repository of books to a place for the people of Parkdale to come together — and soon other branches began to emulate her model.

＝◆＝

RITA COX HAS been bestowed with honour after honour for her work with the Toronto Public Library system. In recognition of her never-ending commitment to collect and make accessible the stories of her people, the Rita Cox Collection of Caribbean Literature was assembled at four different libraries in Toronto. In 1997 she was named to the Order of Canada. In 2000 she was appointed Citizen Court Judge and given the authority to examine and approve landed immigrants for citizenship — a job she takes extremely personally, being an immigrant herself.

If anybody had told Rita as a child that that she would one day end up in Canada, or be the country's Librarian of the Year, or work with scientists on storytelling techniques, or be honoured at a ceremony by Austin Clarke, or stand on stage with the band Rush to receive the highest Canadian honour, she would have been at a loss for words. All she knows is that she loves reading, writing, and speaking — and that by doing what she believes in, she can accomplish great things, like turning a child into a good student. Her mother used to tell her about destiny — what will be will be. Rita's view is that, just as stories need to be told before they can be heard, nothing can happen in life unless you make it happen.

STEVE DIAMOND

There is no getting around the fact that every city has to accommodate growth. It is a much more difficult task than it seems. For example, some European cities, like Paris or London, are now in a situation where they have barely any single-family residential neighbourhoods at their centres; the ones that do exist consist of properties that cost millions of dollars for a few hundred square feet of space. Toronto, on the other hand, is moving in a positive direction. Despite the fact that it has been one of the fastest growing municipalities in North America since the 1950s, it is one of the very few that has single-family neighbourhoods all the way down to the centre of the city, allowing many to get to their jobs without having to commute.

The difference isn't just that Toronto has good developers and a strong political history of engaged residents. It's that it has people like Steve Diamond who help to facilitate the right kind of growth. As former head of the municipal and environmental law department at McCarthy Tétrault, Steve helped modernize the approach towards development in Toronto by his clients, the community, and even the city's planning department. Because of his urging, developers now think more broadly about what buildings are appropriate and where they're appropriate.

What was different about Steve as a development lawyer was that he pushed his clients on the issues, while also pushing the city to think more broadly. Diamond helped to make the debate about development in the city more sophisticated and modern. Instead of letting questions about density be the sole determinant of good planning, Steve pushed elected officials — including me — to look at issues like design and benefits to the community as tests of appropriateness.

Without the reform that he pushed for, the Minto Tower at Yonge and Eglinton would have never been built, paying dividends for the area — nor would residential growth have occurred in the Yorkville and Bloor Street area, leading to one of the finest retail streets in North America.

⟨⟩

STEVE WAS INTRODUCED to development by his father, who had worked in the industry for years as chairman of the board and then CEO of the Cadillac-Fairview Corporation, and would often discuss the issues and controversies related to his job at the dinner table. When Steve grew into a rebellious teenager, he would read negative headlines about new developments — often ones his father was heading up — and question his dad about whether they were doing the right thing. One specific example was a proposal to develop high-rise buildings in the High Park area. Despite the fact that the buildings provided a lot of desperately needed housing, Cadillac-Fairview came up against vehement opposition from the public and from local politicians, and the project was never completed.

His father once told him that he had spent his entire life trying to convince people that development and growth were positive, but never felt he achieved that goal. Young Steve learned that, no matter what the nature of the project was, development in the Toronto core was always going to be controversial. He wanted to be a part of the process.

Steve pursued a career in law, and got his start at Goodman and Goodman. After three years, he took a bold step and left to begin his own law firm. After another ten years, he received a pitch from McCarthy Tétrault to work in their municipal and environmental law department. Though at that point he was running a thriving practice with many clients, Steve accepted the offer. His current job had become increasingly about the money, and his social conscience demanded he contribute to the life of the city in more important ways.

It was not long before Steve ran into the same public opinion issues his father had had to deal with. Every community meeting he attended would usually result in residents objecting to new developments. The city might want a development and the planning department might recommend it and the city council might approve it, but if two hundred people came out to oppose the project, and the city moved forward regardless, it would appear to the community that its voice was not being heard.

Part of the problem, Steve explains, is that many residents do

not understand what the city policies mean, and develop a false expectation of what can and cannot happen in the neighbourhoods they move into. Another key issue is that many of the city's bylaws are outdated. Zoning that was determined decades ago no longer fits into what Toronto needs, yet when a project is discussed, the community points to these old bylaws, whereas the city reviews each project based on potential.

What constitutes "good development" in Toronto? Ask Steve, and you are in for an earful. His metric is formidable: development is "good" if it provides public benefits, and any development ought to be judged on this basic principle alone. Is it going to contribute to the architectural landscape of the city? Is it going to activate the streetscape? Is it going to provide additional housing? What is it going to do in terms of the city's tax base? Employment base? Is it going to promote environmental benefits by being located where people do not have to rely on cars all the time? And will it add to the vibrancy of the city? These are the fundamentals that you take and weigh against any possible negative impacts to the city or the neighbourhood.

Steve is sympathetic to residents' concerns and has enjoyed relatively good relationships with ratepayers groups. But he also discovered there was a gap between how City Hall envisioned development downtown and the direction developers were going. Neither were to blame, they just needed to be challenged about where their visions diverged. His role was to find a way to harmonize the objectives of the developer with the objectives of the City of Toronto. He still has trouble, however, convincing some people that growth is necessary. These are people who would prefer to keep the city much smaller, because they believe that by stopping development, they can prevent change from coming to their neighbourhoods. It doesn't help that most local politicians default to the side of the community because supporting developers usually won't get them re-elected. It takes great courage to embrace an unpopular idea. Fortunately, there are the rare councillors who understand growth cannot be stopped, and can be accommodated in ways that will make everyone proud.

Steve believes he has become such a credible broker between the city and the developers because of his ethics. By constantly doing what he feels is in the public's best interest, Steve has positioned himself in the middle ground, able to question all sides fairly and equally. He has many ideas on what constitutes good development, but only one underlying principle: first and foremost, the development must be of benefit to the public. If the project contributes to the city's architectural landscape, or provides additional housing or jobs, or promotes the environment by creating a location easily accessible for people without cars, he will take those factors into account when weighing the pros and cons.

Because Steve rewarded those who committed to his vision by fighting for their proposals to build taller buildings, Toronto developers began to adhere to his higher standards. Soon, they began to bring in not only some of the finest architects in North America, but creative ideas from all over the world.

❖

AT THIS POINT in his career, Steve is searching for ways to marry private and public concerns in a more direct fashion. He is the chair for PAYE, the Partnership to Advance Youth Employment, which is devoted to helping youth find jobs in the private sector. It is an incredibly moving experience for him to hear how the program has helped change the lives of young people. He believes that what he is doing is vital — the city needs to help its young people achieve their potential, otherwise its future is bleak. And in that sense, Steve's work at PAYE is just a continuation of what he has been doing all his life: helping Toronto grow — the right way.

TOM HEINTZMAN

Tom Heintzman is from the storied Toronto family that founded Heintzman & Co., the piano manufacturer that dominated the Canadian market for over a hundred years, and was responsible for the development of much of the west end of Toronto. I met Tom in early 1977 when his father, a partner at McCarthy Tétrault, one of the most prominent Canadian law firms, interviewed me for Harvard. He was a young, well-scrubbed boy in the junior school at Upper Canada College. Tom Heintzman had every traditional opportunity open to him, but has turned these opportunities down. Instead he has embraced a risky occupation — that of an environmental entrepreneur. Tom founded the first green energy company in Ontario: Bullfrog Power, a company whose business model is best summed up by the phrase, "pay more to do the right thing for the environment." It has been an overwhelming success.

THE FIRST INFLUENTIAL environmentalist in Tom's life was his grandmother. He remembers spending afternoons in the kitchen of her Toronto home, helping her to crush cans before gathering them up and taking them to recycling centres. At the time, he only saw it as an opportunity to bond with a loved one; only later did he realize how unique it was in the seventies for them to be recycling together. His grandmother was a war bride who knew the importance of never wasting a thing — a lesson she imparted to her grandson. More importantly, Tom learned from watching his grandmother that it takes individual effort and commitment to make a difference.

The fossil fuel shortages of the seventies further deepened young Tom's interest in environmental issues. As he watched what was happening in America, with countless cars forming long line-ups to the pump, it struck him how senseless it was that people had allowed themselves to become so dependent on fossil fuels. He was inspired to create a scrapbook for his grade five social science class at UCC, and filled it with articles on wind and solar energy, oil spills, and other far-reaching issues.

In the Trudeau era of the 1970s, Tom's parents were themselves becoming involved in activism. The family would discuss social and political issues at the dinner table, providing material for his already growing social conscience. But it was not until he attended Harvard himself that Tom saw his conscience put to the test. He was surrounded by people who seemed to be active in political issues, but, in his view, were not genuine about it. Many of the undergraduates would rage at government and corporations for their first three years, only to later put on suits and ties and apply for jobs at the very companies they'd been protesting.

At the end of his fourth year, Tom decided to change this trend of what he considered "campus activism." He banded together with his roommates to form the Harvard Radcliffe Students for Corporate Responsibility. They assembled a pamphlet evaluating the corporate practices of businesses that were coming to recruit Harvard students, and included interviews with executives that provided choice quotes for posters, which they then plastered across campus. It was an action that was sure to cause controversy during the ultra-capitalist eighties. Sure enough, the group was hauled into the Dean's office for questioning. Though it was determined that everything they wrote was accurate and that they should not be sanctioned, the campaign had ensured that Tom and his friends were known as radicals.

Tom spent the following year travelling from Alaska to Bolivia. He was particularly interested in the wars taking place in Central American countries like Nicaragua, El Salvador, Guatemala, and Honduras — armed conflicts funded by the Americans to overthrow popularly elected governments. History was taking place, and he wanted to see it as it happened.

One particular incident in Guatemala resonated with him. The group he was travelling with was captured by a militia and taken to a holding station. On the side of one of the barracks was graffiti that said, "If I attack follow me, if I'm captured free me, if I retreat shoot me." He realized he was contending with issues much bigger and more fundamental than the ones on campus, and was inspired to see first hand just how far people were willing to go for what they believed in.

While he was still in Guatemala, Tom applied, and was accepted, to the law school at McGill. In advance of the program, he and his friend Duff Conacher went to Montreal in 1986 in order to start a Public Interest Research Group. PIRG was something that Conacher had learned about while working with Ralph Nader. They held a meeting on the lawn of the law school and introduced the idea of a self-imposed fee for the student body, which would pay for staff and resources for PIRG. That spring, twenty thousand students voted in favour of the fee and the following year picked issues to work on. Their first initiative was a campus-based recycling program, where students would spend weekends sorting paper for a recycling company to take away. Due to the group's initial success at McGill, it expanded to other campuses in Quebec; six years later, it was the largest public interest group in the province.

After graduating from McGill, Tom returned to Toronto to follow in his footsteps and litigate what he called "downtown law cases" — mostly financial, mostly unsatisfying. After five years of working on Bay Street, he felt the need to pursue work he was actually passionate about, and moved on to establish a law firm dealing specifically with environmental issues. Yet, even after doing work with Greenpeace, and winning big cases against Petro-Canada and other corporations, Tom felt like he still wasn't making a big enough impact on the system. He left the practice of law and worked first for McKinsey & Company — one of the largest consultancies in the world — and then ZENON Environmental, a Canadian water purification company with ambitious plans to expand in China and India.

Tom still felt that something was missing. He wanted the ability to influence the speed of environmental change. A particular memory from university stood out: once, while in California, he encountered a school bus painted in psychedelic colours belonging to a retailer of entirely green electricity. Alternative energy companies were unheard of in the late eighties, when most people could not

conceive of being able to choose where they bought their power from; but perhaps now the market was different. As fate would have it, Greg Kiessling — a colleague from McKinsey — was thinking the same thing. They began discussing the possibility of developing solutions for renewable power, and on November 29, 2004, founded Bullfrog Power together. The concept was simple: buy energy from hydro and wind power producers, and sell it to homes and businesses.

The effect on communities was measurable and immediate: the town of Caledon agreed to purchase power through Bullfrog in an attempt to reduce its greenhouse gas emissions by twenty per cent by 2013. It discovered that it was able to reduce its carbon footprint by 142 tonnes of greenhouse gas emissions per year.

Tom was finally in a position where his efforts were having an immediate effect on the environment, something he'd dreamed of doing since he was a student. Tom believed Bullfrog could unlock the enthusiasm of consumers for the central idea that sustainable energy mattered, and he quotes Seth Godin's philosophies frequently in this regard. To paraphrase: if you build something that is truly remarkable then you don't have to do the advertising for it; people will do that for you.

—◆—

BULLFROG POWER STANDS out as an alternative in the Canadian energy economy that has been built upon a long tradition of large energy plants — in an urban area like Toronto, from fossil fuels or nuclear generation — rather than the distributed energy of hundreds of green sources like solar and wind. In Ontario today, the main source of green power is hydro. Unfortunately, the pricing of green power reflects its lack of availability. Although the new Green Energy Act will help create new sources of power in Ontario, until very recently, it simply cost much more to buy green power. Imagine owning a business where you can succeed only if people are willing to pay more for your product!

Despite those challenges, Bullfrog is succeeding. Environmental responsibility is slowly shifting from governments and corporations to households and individuals. The company now offers Canadians in six provinces one hundred per cent renewable electricity. In just five years it has grown to roughly eight thousand homes and one thousand businesses. As people become more aware of where their energy comes from and the environmental and health costs associated with conventional energy, they are making switches on various levels — people are also choosing non-toxic cleaners, greener detergents, hybrid vehicles. Bullfrog Power is proof that people are beginning to understand — just like Tom and his family — that when change is needed, they must choose to make it happen.

MEHRAN BERMAH

At the intersection of James and Albert streets, tucked in behind Old City Hall and facing the southwest doors of the Eaton Centre, is a hot dog stand belonging to Mehran Bermah. Mehran is not an ordinary hot dog vendor; he's a bit of a philosopher. His customers return not only for the hot sausages and Bavarian-style wieners and cold drinks, but also for his conversation, his observations about life in Toronto, and his engagement with the people he sees. It's easy to see why, for some people, Mehran has become one of their daily touchstones — a moment shared with him reminds them where exactly they are.

MEHRAN'S PHILOSOPHICAL TURN comes out of his life's experience. He grew up in Iran, on his father's farm near the Caspian Sea. His father had three wives and fourteen children. Although he remembers the family having little money, Mehran does not remember them as poor; he does remember, however, that they felt distinctly that they were not from the city. On the farm, his father grew corn and rice and raised chickens. The young Mehran watched his father and understood his work ethic; he saw the relationship between a person's work and the sense of identity that comes from it.

As an adult, Mehran experienced success of his own. He owned a chicken farm, a fabric store, and a rice store. The farm was large and productive, employing fifty workers. His stores did well and their profits made it possible for him to buy a piece of land, as well as a small house in northern Iran.

Trouble lay on the horizon, however. Similar to running a business in Canada, running businesses in Iran required proper registrations and permits. Mehran had not had his registrations and permits validated with the proper stamps — an infraction that, in Iran, was punishable by thirty lashings in public.

Mehran was found in violation of Law 86 — the law pertaining to proper business documentation — and tried in court. The process was unclear and the explanations for the law were not forthcoming; evidently, the justice system was focused only on the punishment. Mehran was not permitted to defend himself, nor given the opportunity to inform the court that he lived honestly, did not smoke or drink, and observed all other Muslim laws. The judge did not appear to concern himself with Mehran's character either.

After suffering the force of the lashings in public, Mehran developed a hatred for Iranian laws. He was hurt and, worse, humiliated. These events destroyed his life in the country of his birth, leading

him to leave Iran in 1989 for Brussels, where he lived for a time. He eventually came to Toronto, where through luck alone he landed one of the best pieces of vendor real estate in the city.

When he first arrived in Toronto in 1994, Mehran did not speak English adequately, so he enrolled in ESL classes within weeks, and studied the language for six months. When he felt he had enough English under his belt to make conversation possible, he bought the licence for a hot dog stand located at 100 St. George Street. Unfortunately, he'd bought the wrong permit. His licence was cancelled soon after. Mehran went to City Hall and discovered that he had been sold a bill of goods: not only had the seller given him the wrong sticker for the permit, he had convinced Mehran to buy the location itself — a purchase that was completely unnecessary. The City Hall clerk who listened to Mehran was not only understanding, but compassionate, and instrumental in turning his misfortune into good luck. The clerk was able to direct him to a licence for a location just outside the Eaton Centre, arguably one of the busier hot dog stands in the city. Good fortune was finally smiling upon him, and he seized the opportunity.

⟨═⟩

IF YOU ASK him today how he likes his work, Mehran will tell you that he loves it. And yet, the stand requires serious effort. His hours are nine a.m. to nine p.m., all week. At six a.m. he picks up his ice, loads his inventory, and heads to Old City Hall. This is his daily routine for all but forty-eight days a year. From mid-January to the beginning of March, Mehran returns to Iran to check on the property he still owns there, and to see his brothers and sisters.

Going back to Iran causes Mehran to feel mixed emotions. Although it is much different today than twenty-three years ago, he still does not feel safe when he's there. He comments that the "better" times in Iran have made people forget the worse times and that the young people have no awareness of how limited life was in the early days, after the revolution.

Once he gets talking about Canada and Canadians, Mehran becomes a philosopher. Canada means freedom to Mehran — freedom to be able to talk to people, freedom to set his own rules at work, freedom to live the life he chooses. He believes that being Canadian means being motivated. He compares his life with his brothers' and wonders aloud if they would be willing to sell hot dogs on the street in minus-thirty-degree temperatures. He's pretty sure they wouldn't — he jokes that they're lazy. But his good-natured differences with his siblings are merely familial play; he reserves his judgments for Canadians who don't appreciate the gifts they have. He explains that the reason for this complacency is too much freedom. Having never experienced tyranny, most Canadians don't recognize the value of the freedoms they take for granted.

Mehran has many stories of customers who've held forth with him on a variety of subjects. He recalls one man who was outraged by the extensive and expensive renovations to Old City Hall. The man was angry that public money was being wasted on old buildings. Without waiting a moment, Mehran responded to the man by explaining that old buildings represented history, Canadian history, and because of this they mattered. He told the man that not only were his eyes closed, but his mind, too; all he had to do was look around to see how beautiful Toronto and Canada were.

It's this kind of philosophizing and connecting that have turned some of Mehran's customers into family. His stand has become a meeting place where people share their observations and troubles with him and he shares his with them. It's his informal university and, in his opinion, it's the best in the world. Nowhere else will he learn as much as he learns every day at the intersection of James and Albert streets.

Mehran is willing to share some of the lessons he has learned. His favourite stories are about reading faces — something not taught in universities. In one story, an American tourist stops to buy a hot dog and Mehran tells him that his bill comes to twenty-nine dollars: four dollars for the hot dog and pop, twenty-five dollars for the tip. The American comments on the alarming exchange rate, pays him, and laughs. Mehran notes that when he sees the fellow again, if he does, they'll be like brothers. In another story, a young man asks for a can of ginger ale, but when he reaches in his pocket he realizes he doesn't have the cash to buy the drink. Mehran tells him not to worry, to take the pop anyway. He trusts that the young man will return with the money — which he does, twenty minutes later, giving Mehran a fifty-cent tip. Mehran explains that he could see the young man's honesty in his face, and that he has faith in his fellow man.

His experiences with the law in Iran have not tainted his faith. As a Muslim he believes in God and he believes that his religion informs who he is. He observes the fasting of Ramadan and has been to Mecca, Medina, and Jeddah. He wishes that his customers understood what his fasting means to him, and that his visits to the holy cities of Islam are profoundly transformative.

Reflecting upon his life, and the events that brought him to this juncture, Mehran says that perhaps selling hot dogs isn't the life he would have chosen for himself — perhaps he should have found a better job. But selling hot dogs is the life he has and he intends to continue giving it his best. He believes that no one dies from hard work — and he believes that the right path to take in life just might be the hard way, if it makes him wiser, and if it takes him longer. Like many immigrants, he works hard to ensure that he does better than his father and that his sons do better than he. He says he never wants to retire because he wouldn't know what to do without the daily contact with his customers — he'd lose the conversation that is his life. His life's work is his life's pleasure, and he was reminded of this on his most recent return from Iran. At Pearson Airport, the customs officers welcomed him "home" and he burst into tears. He realized that, after sixteen years, he loves Toronto and that it is his home.

WILLIAM BOYD

Most Torontonians have had the experience of walking by a homeless person on the streets of our city at one time or another. Some have also had the experience of chatting with someone who is street-involved; only a few have had the chance to get to know street-involved homeless people as persons — as fellow Torontonians.

The City of Toronto's approach to street-involved homeless people starts with that powerful idea: that someone living on the streets of our city *is* a fellow Torontonian, and has his or her own story. Our program, Streets to Homes, was one of my most important achievements in my first term as mayor. Trained social workers are sent to meet homeless people to get to know them and their needs — job training, income support, addiction counselling, and of course permanent housing. Once the person is ready, housing is found and follow-up support is provided for their needs. Streets to Homes has helped over two thousand people into permanent housing — almost all of whom are still living in that housing. The program is so successful it has won awards from the United Nations. But the biggest award is in the results: the last census showed that the number of people living on the streets of Toronto since the introduction of Streets to Homes has dropped by half.

⋯◆⋯

ALTHOUGH A DIFFERENT program helped William Boyd, his story is similar to that of many homeless people. He has learned some hard lessons in his time. His family arrived in Canada on May 6, 1956, from the small town of Ballymena in the northern part of Ireland. He was thirteen when they arrived and was enrolled in grade nine at Vaughan Road Collegiate Institute. Later he transferred to Humberside Collegiate in Toronto's Bloor West area. He emerged from high school in 1960 having specialized in two areas: music (he was a drummer) and girls. He had absolutely no idea what he wanted to do for a living and was walking along Bloor Street one day when he saw a "help wanted" sign in the window of his local bank. He went in, talked to the manager, and days later started his career working as a junior teller. Little did he know he was embarking upon a personal odyssey that would last twenty-five years and end in total burnout, nervous breakdown, and, eventually, the loss of family, friends, and everything he owned.

From a junior teller, Boyd moved quickly up the chain. He had the gift of the gab and was as charismatic then as he is today, complete with a movie-star smile. Soon he had managed five different bank branches in the city, heading up a capital finance division in the city, and running a commercial development department out west. The young Irish boy had graduated to the top of his game, and his days were often filled with client meetings and big lunches; it was a world where material things were very important, and egos often clashed. William had all the bells and whistles: big cars, second properties, even a boat. But after twenty-five years in the banking business the stress finally caught up with him and in 1985 he suffered a nervous breakdown at his desk — something he now describes as a "spiritual emergency" — brought on by severe anxiety and depression. He felt totally burned out and it culminated one afternoon when he showed at head office intending to resign. It did not help his confidence to discover they had already prepared his walking papers.

After walking away from his twenty-five-year career that afternoon, William started seeing a psychologist and decided to complete his real estate licence; in hindsight, the latter was a mistake — it just brought on new stresses. So he packed up and went north to Penetanguishene and used the severance he'd received from the bank to buy himself a cottage to fix up. It was an oasis away from the city where he did a lot of reading and meditating. But the comfort was false, and he eventually experienced a massive breakdown, which landed him in the hospital in 1989 after he threw his TV set and most of the contents of his cottage off the deck.

Boyd was diagnosed with manic depression and put on lithium, which he says made him a zombie. He was trying to rebuild his life but the stigma associated with mental illness weighed him down and he went through two marriages between 1986 and 1996. He opened a little bookstore in Penetanguishine called The Labyrinth, which specialized in spiritual books, and spent most of his days in the shop reading through its contents. Then in 1999 his mother

fell ill and was placed on life support in hospital. He arrived to visit one day and was devastated to find that orders had been given to disconnect her. William became agitated and phoned the police but that landed him back in hospital in restraints and under observation. His mother died a few days later. He was not allowed to attend her funeral.

He was eventually released, but didn't like the dulled-down effect the medicine was producing; he'd lost the sparkle in his life, so he eventually refused to continue taking his medicine and chose to go it alone. Rather than burden his family, whose patience he felt he'd already pushed, Boyd packed some belongings and ended up homeless on the streets of Toronto. He remembers dwelling on his many regrets, a process he describes now as a kind of "self-psychoanalysis." At the same time he was learning the rules of the street — one of the most important and challenging being "always mind your own business." Having been a bank manager, it was second nature for him to ask in-depth questions, and this sometimes got him in trouble.

Amid his ongoing spiritual crisis, there were practical questions of day-to-day living on the street: Where do I go? Where will I sleep? What will I eat? Boyd never panhandled; he still had a little money saved up but he needed to find ways to fill his days. William occasionally passed time by sitting in on council meetings and listening to the proceedings. One day, while he was searching out City Hall's washrooms, among the more comfortable places he would use to clean up a bit, he found the inside facilities were out of service and under temporary construction, while those outside were not only filthy, but their doors were hanging off. He walked upstairs and into the mayor's office to lodge a complaint. He asked if he could use the washroom there and remembers how pleased he was at being treated like a normal person.

He lived on the streets through all four seasons, spending days and months wandering, and a lot of time on his own. This came to an abrupt end when he was arrested for getting in a parked car with the keys in the ignition to warm up. That got him five days in solitary confinement, something he does not want to ever relive; however, his court case was thrown out. His experience put him in touch with a program called Homeward, which was designed to help people off the streets and into subsidized housing. He lives in the same place today, five years later.

By living on the street, William feels he learned, more than anything else, how to empathize. He feels he always had this quality as a bank manager but the street experience further awakened it in him. He saw a lot of people who were also genuinely lost. Walking in their shoes and going through the same things they had gone through was humbling. The result of his spiral down was the loss of all his material possessions, but he finds it strange how, now that they're gone, he doesn't really miss them. Now, more than anything, he longs to get to know his grandson, whom he has never met, and he wishes to reunite with his son, from whom he's been estranged for almost two decades.

⟨⟩

BOYD HAD THE luck of the Irish and then lost it. But he's been able to find it again in simple pleasures. To remind himself of easier days, he plays Irish melodies on a type of bass whistle known as a flageolet. His journey has taught him there are a lot of people on the street who are just like him: all they need is someone to sit down with them and talk with them, ask what they can do to help, and give them a bit of guidance on how to get out of the labyrinth they're going through. When he was young all he wanted to do was get ahead — "more money, more parties, more toys" — but it all catches up to you. William still owns a suit, but has long since traded his quest for money for a spiritual one. Instead of immersing himself in banking literature and a morning conference call, he now practises formal meditation and is extremely well-read on the yogic teachings of Kundalini. His breakdown helped awaken a spiritual mechanism in his body that he feels has accelerated his mystical journey.

In the end he feels indebted to his experience on Toronto's streets because it taught him things about himself. He believes the power of conversation is important in helping homeless people off the streets and he wants to give this gift back to the city that taught him one of the most important lessons in his life: to empathize is to be human. William says soul-searching has been a major aspect of his spiritual journey. He still walks the streets of Toronto from time to time because it allows him to think things through. He recommends it to everybody.

JOHN KOUROGIORGAS

On the western edge of Bloor West Village, six blocks west of the north entrance to High Park, sits a diner called the Bloor Jane Restaurant. Bustling during the week and even busier on weekends, its lineups — featuring frequent customers, weekend walkers, and even the occasional celebrity — often grow so long they spill out the door and onto the sidewalk. Its regulars come from all walks of life: it would not be unusual for a street person to wait for breakfast next to politicians or stockbrokers, or for an NHL hockey player to enjoy a meal alongside local school kids on lunch break. Thanks to its loyal customers, it has withstood economic downturns and competition from chains like Tim Hortons and McDonald's, and has kept its doors open for thirty-eight years and counting. For at least twenty of those years, I have been a customer.

Boasting a storied history, famous clientele, and vintage fifties décor, the Bloor Jane is without a doubt a beacon of my neighbourhood, but the most remarkable thing about the diner might be its owner, John Kourogiorgas.

⸺◆⸺

JOHN, OR "JOHNNY K," as he is known to his regulars, began life on a farm in a small Greek village, where he finished school at grade ten. He spent most of his days afterwards helping his family tend to their olive trees, orange trees, and cotton plants.

By his middle teen years, John was already a romantic. He drew inspiration from the rich heritage of Greece and its position as the seat of western civilization. But, more than anything, it was his love of North American movies that would have the most impact on his future dreams and ambitions. He longed to travel across the Atlantic in hope of seeing more movies, maybe even becoming a star himself one day. With a sister living in Toronto, Canada became his destination of choice.

When he turned sixteen and suddenly found himself two years away from mandatory service in the Greek army, John decided it was time to join his sister overseas, and so, alone, he boarded a ship bound for Canada and for ten days fought off seasickness caused by the torrential conditions during the crossing. On January 27, 1962, his ship pulled into Halifax Harbour. He remembers being frozen to the bone, but happy to be there.

His sister and her husband greeted him on the platform at Union Station after his train rolled in from Halifax. They took him back to their place on Olive Street. Of all his memories of that day, the most vivid is his first streetcar ride up Bathurst Street. Seeing the streets paved in red brick was, for him, like arriving on a different planet.

John's brother-in-law allowed him one week of down time; after that, he had to find work. A tip led him to Solway Delicatessen, near Bay and Bloor, where he applied for a job as a dishwasher. Thanks to his "Pepsi smile," they hired him on the spot. He took classes to learn English. Over the following months, he slowly moved up to delivery boy, and from there to waiter. After only three years of working at Solway, he and his brother bought the place outright. He was only eighteen and already the owner of a business.

In his early days, John was fascinated by television. It was something that had been completely unknown to him in Greece. He still remembers watching the moon landing and coverage of the Kennedy assassination. But most of John's off-hours were spent experiencing as much of Toronto as possible. The delicatessen gave him the perfect vantage point. From behind his counter, he watched in fascination as the influence of beatniks, motorcycle gangs, movie stars, the Beatles, the Rolling Stones, and Elvis Presley flooded Yorkvillle. The nonstop cultural activity of the sixties marks it as his favourite decade of his life.

The deli also gave John a chance to personally participate in the city scene. He was thrilled to meet the Canadian actors who worked at the Scollard Street studio around the corner. Close proximity to Maple Leaf Gardens meant Leafs players such as Dick Duff and Mike Walton would drop in. Serving them inspired in John a passion for hockey that continues to this day. The Gardens became a regular stop for him, especially for games played on Saturday nights. He was in attendance, too, when the Beatles played their legendary show there, although he recalls being unable to hear a thing over the roar of the crowd.

In 1970, John went back to Greece for a year of holiday. He remembers thinking at the time that he was still young and perhaps should find a wife. So motivated, he met a girl at an Astros beach

and romanced her until the time came to return to Toronto and run his restaurant. Their parting was melancholy, but it was not long-lived; she joined him in Canada six months later.

People are often surprised to hear that John is married — he doesn't bring his wife or kids to the restaurant. His customers often ask him how he can work seven days a week and have a family. The key, he tells them, is to keep family separate from business. He gets all his work done at the diner, including the paperwork, so that when he goes home he leaves his work behind. He has not advised either of his daughters to follow in his footsteps, but both are business-minded, and one owns and operates a bridal boutique in Oakville. Neither can believe that he ran his own business when he was so young.

When the lease ended at the Bay and Bloor location in 1972, John and his brother moved to a diner at Jane and Bloor that had been operated by a couple of fellow Greeks since 1955. They saw that the place retained its original fifties look and resolved to not change a thing. It turned out to be a wise decision. Although Bloor West in the 1970s was not as busy as Yorkville in the sixties, especially on weekends, the new location quickly came into its own, and the stories that emerged would match those of the Solway Delicatessen.

Hockey, John's adopted love, has much to do with Bloor Jane's history. He installed a television in the diner for the first time to watch the Summit Series in 1972. Later, he caught a familiar face looking through the front window at a hockey stick hanging on the wall; it was Leaf hero Börje Salming, who then came inside and autographed the stick. John has made a standing promise to throw a free breakfast party when the Leafs win the Stanley Cup. While this has yet to take place, one of his patrons provided the next best thing. The man, who was related to the owner of the Detroit Red Wings, promised John a Christmas present he would never forget:

the Stanley Cup itself. And sure enough, on a Monday afternoon a few years ago, the Cup was brought to Bloor Jane and set in the front booth. John watched as they removed it from its special case, and for the two hours the trophy was with him, he marvelled at the names of the legendary players inscribed upon it, and revelled in memories of his friends from the Leaf teams of the sixties.

Television, too, has made its mark on the Bloor Jane. The media seem to appreciate the diner's unique setup, one eschewing chairs and tables for a counter and booths. A broadcast of *Breakfast Television*, featuring special guest musician Jeff Healey, was once shot in the restaurant. An exception was made in that case: generally, John turns down shooting requests, even when large fees are offered to make up for lost business, because he prefers not to close his doors to customers.

It is this sort of commitment that explains why Bloor Jane has been so successful for so long. John believes that his job, first and foremost, is to work as hard as possible to serve the people. That means anything from using the best quality ingredients, to hiring the perfect servers — in almost forty years he's only had four — to saying hello to every customer who comes in. His work ethic and hospitality are certainly appreciated in the community. The diner has never been robbed, even though the cash register sits right next to the window. The bank on the corner has been robbed several times. Once, a customer who forgot to pay for breakfast later sent John a Christmas card with a twenty enclosed.

⊫⊶

NOTHING LASTS FOREVER, unfortunately. John has begun lately to think about retirement, which is strange for a man who has only ever taken Christmas and New Year's Day off, and who got married at home so he could be at work the next day. Money is not his main concern. Although margins are slim, John has made enough to retire comfortably, send his two daughters to school, and even buy a second property to rent out. What he will miss the most about the job, he believes, are the people. He has grown attached to his customers, having interacted with them almost every day for thirty-eight years.

But when all is said and done, John thinks he will be content when he finally sells the Bloor Jane Diner. The first thing he will do is return to Greece and the beach at Astros where his dream of coming to Toronto was first conceived, and enjoy the knowledge that, with a lot of hard work and a little courtesy, he was able to make his dream come true.

THE HUMBER RIVER
PEDESTRIAN CYCLING BRIDGE

My favourite place in Toronto is a bridge — the precisely named Humber River Pedestrian Cycling Bridge. No matter how busy I am, I run, bike, or walk there at least once a week; when I am in serious training I run across it several times a week. It is a place of great beauty, and for me, great solitude. When I need moments of calm reflection — as I needed in order to craft the speech I gave announcing that I would not be running in the 2010 municipal election — it is to the bridge that I go. In fact, I crafted that speech in my head during successive runs along Toronto's waterfront, always across the bridge, and when it was finished, simply dictated it to my staff. Such is the peace to be found on the bridge that the speech I gave was changed only in very minor ways from the one that came to me on the bridge.

ONE OF THE astonishing qualities of the Humber River Bridge is how calm it is in the middle of the span. It does not matter what the weather, there is a serenity that invites you to pause and savour the amazing view east across Toronto's waterfront to downtown, or to look north up the Humber River. Even in the midst of a driving snowstorm I have stopped to savour the feeling of peace. To me, the peace comes from the design, and from the historic importance of the mouth of the river as the foot of the Carrying Place Trail. The soaring arches, reinforced by giant symbolic thunderbirds, give the passerby a sense of welcome and security. This may be because Native artists and elders were involved in the symbolism of the design features. Descriptions of the bridge say, "The structure metaphorically bridges water and sky, earth and air, human and prehistoric time." The design — by Montgomery and Sisan Architects of Toronto and Delcan Corporation — has won numerous prestigious architectural and engineering awards, and is a testament to the fact that public buildings can and should be designed for beauty. But the extraordinary design is only the most visible thing about the bridge.

To me, the Humber River Bridge brings together the best of our city and its people. First of all, the bridge was instrumental in returning the water's edge to the people of Toronto. Sunnyside, Palais Royale, and nearby Palace Pier historically were the site of tremendous recreation and entertainment opportunities for Torontonians. They were reachable by streetcar and by two nearby train stations, including the Bolt Works station at the then-factory (later owned by Stelco) at Windermere and the Queensway. Thousands of Torontonians sought their entertainment at Sunnyside — and cooled off from the hot summer weather at its beaches. Postwar, Sunnyside began to decline, and with the advent of the Gardiner Expressway — and the tearing up of the streetcar tracks — Sunnyside died, cut

off from Parkdale and from the people of Toronto. Palace Pier was closed and razed; Palais Royale fell into virtual disuse until being rejuvenated while I was mayor. Some private facilities remained and thrived — like the Boulevard Club, which occupies prime waterfront land for an elite-members-only facility. But public lands suffered from a lack of investment and they, and their use, declined.

In the late 1980s and early 1990s, the City of Toronto recognized the past and the future potential of Sunnyside and built a wonderful boardwalk along the water's edge, constructed from a material made out of recycled pop bottles. The boardwalk brought back vitality and life to the western beaches — when the water's edge is brought back to the people it always succeeds — and became a roaring success.

=◆=

IT WAS IN this context that the former regional government, the Municipality of Metropolitan Toronto, proposed the rebuilding of the Lakeshore/Gardiner bridges over the Humber River, just north of the mouth. The project was to be part of the first federal infrastructure program and was clearly needed as the bridge abutments had sunk at the river's edge and a famous "bump" appeared in the road. But then an amazing thing happened — residents spoke up. They said, "If you are going to spend over one hundred million dollars serving the needs of those who live outside Toronto, we want our local needs met too." They demanded a pedestrian connection across the mouth of the Humber. Gunnars Martinsons, a local resident and activist with the Swansea Ratepayers, was a wonderfully irascible man fighting for a people's bridge, not just one for cars. To me, this kind of drive represents the best of community activism — fighting for a shared idea of how to build our city for the future. All too often in Toronto we remember to fight against something, but forget how to build a truly great city.

In this case, the community won: the road bridges were redesigned to save money, and the savings used to pay for the pedestrian cycling bridge — with millions of dollars involved. In 1994, the bridge linked the former cities of Etobicoke and Toronto, and since it was built has helped create an explosion in the use of the Martin Goodman Trail both west and east of the Humber. It has opened the west end of Toronto's great waterfront to its residents and visitors in the same way the Carrying Place Trail opened up Lake Ontario to the Native traders and early settlers.

I think one of the reasons I love this bridge so much is that the way it was built also connects that history. The fact that excellence in design and architecture was demanded befits the fact of the mouth of the Humber being the historic start of Toronto. We designed the bridge with the advice of our aboriginal peoples, honouring their heritage in the thunderbirds that frame the view from the bridge deck up to the sky, and in the turtles, snakes, and totemic masks that adorn the bridge, each with their own symbolic importance. The bridge was built with the most advanced construction techniques, including the use of cranes to lift it into place — befitting a city that is home to some of the highest-skilled unionized construction workers in the world, and some of the best contractors. It symbolizes the idea that investment in public goods, and the public realm, permanently benefits all of us. At a time when the political landscape has been too shaped by the ideology of Reagan and Thatcher — that no government is good government, and all taxes are bad — the Humber River Bridge stands for the idea that public investments in great public places have enduring value, and that public money can and should be invested in beautiful places that benefit all of us.

There is another reason I love this bridge — a personal one. One of the first duties I had as a Metro councillor was to cut the ribbon on the bridge. There were many dignitaries there, but somehow I managed to be the first person to officially cross the bridge. And I have never stopped.

ACKNOWLEDGEMENTS

This book was a collaboration between me, Jeff Davidson, and Doug Arrowsmith. I want to acknowledge and thank them for their hard work and shared insights. Jules Koostachin and Nithiya Neduncharalathan transcribed the interviews, and the team at Cormorant Books provided superb editing, sound advice, and from the beginning had confidence in my vision for this book. Most of all, I want to thank the Torontonians who have allowed me to share their stories in this book. If there are any errors in the book, the responsibility is mine.

ENVIRONMENTAL BENEFITS STATEMENT

Cormorant Books saved the following resources by printing the pages of this book on chlorine free paper made with 100% post-consumer waste.

TREES	WATER	SOLID WASTE	GREENHOUSE GASES
23	10,662	647	2,214
FULLY GROWN	GALLONS	POUNDS	POUNDS

Calculations based on research by Environmental Defense and the Paper Task Force.
Manufactured at Friesens Corporation